Five Uneasy Pieces

Five Uneasy Pieces

Essays on Law and Evolution

Jan M. Smits

eleven
international publishing

Published, sold and distributed by Eleven International Publishing
P.O. Box 85576
2508 CG The Hague
The Netherlands
Tel.: +31 70 33 070 33
Fax: +31 70 33 070 30
e-mail: sales@elevenpub.nl
www.elevenpub.com

Sold and distributed in USA and Canada
Independent Publishers Group
814 N. Franklin Street
Chicago, IL 60610, USA
Order Placement: +1 800 888 4741
Fax: +1 312 337 5985
orders@ipgbook.com
www.ipgbook.com

Eleven International Publishing is an imprint of Boom uitgevers Den Haag.

ISBN 978-94-6236-982-5
ISBN 978-94-6094-431-4 (E-book)

Cover illustration: Trial by battle as depicted in the 14th century Dresden codex of the *Sachsenspiegel*

Table of Contents

Preface

Introduction

Herman Melville once wrote that it is better to fail in originality than to succeed in imitation. It is a motto I always felt attracted to. Over the last ten years I have published a number of articles in which the law is looked at from an evolutionary perspective. These articles fit Melville's motto particularly well. They do not try to build upon the work of others, or work out ambitious theoretical or doctrinal constructs, but instead attempt to relate different aspects of law to the Darwinian idea of survival of the fittest in (also for me) unexpected ways. This work did not form the core of my academic work in that period, but in hindsight the five articles – although dealing with seemingly different topics – are remarkably similar in their attempt to relate the law to evolutionary ideas.

This preface aims to explain the core idea underlying the five chapters. The idea that law and legal development can be understood as the result of an evolutionary process is not new as such, but in the last century it largely made place for a view that regards law as either the product of a competent authority or as being derived from some transcendent nature or culture. This is remarkable in view of the fact that in recent decades other academic disciplines increasingly build upon evolutionary insights. Some authors even claim that evolutionary theory is the only surviving theory able to explain structural changes regardless of the context in which these changes take place. Be this as it may, this was not the main reason for writing these contributions. I found it highly rewarding to try to relate evolutionary ideas as applied in biology, economics, psychology and linguistics to the law, without any further goal than the pursuit of knowledge. In this sense, this little book is also a plea for what I consider to be the true university: a place for cross-disciplinary teaching and research steered by curiosity.

Adopting an evolutionary perspective means asking questions other than those legal scholars are prone to ask and giving answers that may be unexpected. In writing these contributions, I never felt I had both feet planted on level ground. This also explains the title of this book, with a nod to Richard Feynman's famous *Six Easy Pieces*. Unlike Feynman's work, this book does not explain any essentials, but it does invite the reader to think along and criticize the approach and the conclusions reached in each of the chapters. There is no greater merit in academia than to be criticized. This was also the motto of the late Herman Schoordijk (1926-2018) who, first through his writings and then through numerous conversations, opened up the field of private law for me. To me, his lifelong motto that 'we should not unnecessarily agree' implies that academics should never go for the smooth and the easy and should, most of all, ask their own questions and not the questions others want them to answer.

Law and Evolution: A Survey of the Chapters

The core of evolution through natural selection is that the better adapted organisms are more likely to survive and leave more offspring than the less adapted ones. The application of this idea is not confined to natural organisms or genes, but can also be applied to any other entity capable of mutation and selection. Natural selection only requires a 'replicator', something that can be copied onto a next generation.

Chapter 1 shows that the law fits this framework particularly well. Law is indeed passed on from one generation to the next and, even though profound changes in the law may occur over time, its development is usually seen as a continuous one. Put differently: law is quite literally a *tradition*, a set of principles and rules transmitted from generation to generation. If people follow this tradition, they are more likely to gain the necessary approval of society and thus seek to do better than those who do not follow existing rules. Chapter 1 takes up this point by applying the specific evolutionary framework of 'symbiosism', developed by the Leiden school of linguistics, to the law. The basis for this theory is that language is an organism residing in the human brain and is therefore a memetic life form. The chapter makes the point that law, like language, enhances the Darwinian fitness of the human species. This theory is subsequently used to help explain differences among jurisdictions, in particular why it is that differences continue to exist over time.

Chapter 2 explores how evolutionary insights can be used to explain the convergence of law. It builds upon the debate on harmonization of private law in the European Union, in which a key question is whether cultural and societal differences among the member states stand in the way of reaching similar outcomes on the basis of common texts. It is argued that looking at law as an evolutionary organism can help to explain whether this is the case. Just as organisms are shaped by irreversible transformations in the past, the law is also affected by the path traced out in its previous development. Legal rules are therefore never completely shaped by the needs of their environment, but are also dependent on their own characteristics (their 'nature'). For example, it is likely that transnational commercial law and European contract law are less affected by the factor of nature and therefore more susceptible to change than, for example, property or family law. In addition, legal diversity is likely to decrease in those areas where the environment becomes more uniform, as in the field of international business.

Chapter 3 also takes up the idea that the law, when considered an organism, is a self-adapting system. It looks at law as a complex system and asks whether there is a relationship between the size of a country's population and the complexity of the law. The common assumption is that the law of larger jurisdictions is just as simple or complex as the law of smaller jurisdictions. However, this hypothesis was never empirically tested. This is surprising in view of the fact that a thriving field of research in linguistics deals with the relationship between language complexity and the size of the speech community. This research shows that grammatical complexity correlates negatively with the size of the speech community – the bigger the community, the simpler the grammar. Chapter 3 investigates whether the same is true for the law, drawing materials from both constitutional and private law.

Chapter 4, written together with three undergraduate students at Maastricht University, investigates how the law is perceived in hip-hop music. Lawyers' presuppositions about morality, legality and justice are not always shared by non-lawyers. This chapter offers an inventory and analysis of how the law is seen in the influential English and American hip-hop scene. It is clear that hip-hop lyrics were not written with Darwin in mind, and yet they invariably describe the world as a place where one has to fight in order not to become someone else's prey. The law is an instrument to be used to one's advantage where possible and to be ignored if not useful, and thus a way to survive in the urban jungle.

The final Chapter 5 aims to shed new light on the contested history of the so-called price payment rule. It does so by testing a method of analysis that has until now not been used in analysing legal materials. This method is based on computational phylogenetics, the quantitative study of the evolutionary history of organisms. Computational phylogenetic analysis was originally developed in the field of biology where it is used to evaluate heritable traits, such as DNA sequences, with a view to building trees showing the evolutionary relationships among different species. In this chapter, this method is applied to the rule that makes the transfer of movable property dependent on the buyer's payment of the price. The study provides a dataset of 56 variations of the price payment rule from 41 different jurisdictions drafted between the years 150 and 2006. Using Mesquite, these variations are quantified as phylogenetic trees and subsequently analysed to draw conclusions about their common history.

ACKNOWLEDGEMENTS

This book is partly based upon previously published work. Chapter 1 was published in *Review of Law and Economics* 2011, Chapter 2 in Peer Zumbansen & Gralf-Peter Calliess (eds.), *Law, Economics and Evolutionary Theory*, Cheltenham 2011, Chapter 3 in Alexis Albarian & Olivier Moréteau (eds.), *Le droit compare et.../Comparative Law and...*, Aix-en-Provence 2016 and Chapter 4 (written with my students Andrei Ernst, Steven Iseger and Nida Riaz) in *Ars Aequi* 2013. Thanks are due to the publishers for their consent to republish these contributions here in modified form. Chapter 5 appears for the first time in this book.

The various chapters greatly benefited from help and comments provided by Bram Akkermans, Konstantinos Amiridis, Allison Bilska, William Bull, Julie De Coninck, Peter Cserne, Gijs van Dijck, Seán Patrick Donlan, Jeanne Gaakeer, Kristi Georgieva, Samantha Gernat, Catalina Goanta, Jaap Hage, Bram van Hofstraeten, Karolina Horská, Nelis Karakash, Mark Kawakami, Steven Kelk, Nina Koivula, Amoiridis Konstantinos, Bart Du Laing, Laura Lamster, Tereza Látová, Gary Low, Yanitsa Maksimova, Rodrigo Momberg, Olivier Moréteau, Siskos Nikolaos, Nikol Nikolova, Daniel On, Agustin Parise, Ludwig Ritter, Benedikt Schmitz, Bruno Vieira and Marc Weerts.

I am grateful to the editors of the *Maastricht Law Series* for their willingness to include this title in their series, and to the staff at BoomJuridisch and Eleven International Publishing for their great support.

Maastricht/Liège, September 2019

1 Is Law a Parasite? An Evolutionary Explanation of Differences among Legal Traditions*

1.1 Introduction

One of the most salient characteristics of law (or at least of large parts of it) is that it can be seen as a *tradition*. Law is passed on from one generation to another and, even though profound changes in the law may occur over time, its development is usually seen as a continuous one. Thus, in *The Common Law*, Oliver Wendell Holmes states that "the law embodies the story of a nation's development through many centuries (...)".[1] Alan Watson also emphasizes the extraordinary persistence of the law, noting that similar rules were transplanted from one society to another and were used under Julius Caesar, in the Middle Ages and in the 20th-century welfare society.[2] Particularly in the field of comparative law, this concept of tradition is widely used to distinguish several types of jurisdictions from each other.[3]

It is interesting to note that this phenomenon of law as a tradition has received only little attention in the academic literature seeking to explain differences among jurisdictions.[4] This chapter seeks to remedy this deficiency. Its purpose is to explain the endurance and continuing development of different legal traditions from an evolutionary perspective and thus to contribute to our knowledge of why jurisdictions differ from each other. It does so by applying a specific evolutionary framework that was originally developed by linguists, but the importance of which transcends to the

* Published in Review of Law and Economics 7 (2011) 791-804.

1 O.W. Holmes, *The Common Law* (1881), ed. T.A. Schweich, New York 2004, 1.

2 A. Watson, *Legal Transplants: An Approach to Comparative Law* (Edinburgh 1974), 2nd ed., Athens GA 1993. Cf. W. Ewald, 'Comparative Jurisprudence (II): The Logic of Legal Transplants', *American Journal of Comparative Law* 43 (1995) 489, at 490 and already F. Bacon, *The New Organon and Related Writings* (1620), ed. F.H. Anderson, New York 1960, 89: 'In matters of state a change even for the better is distrusted, because it unsettles what is established; these things resting on authority, consent, fame and opinion, not on demonstration.'

3 Cf. e.g. K. Zweigert & H. Kötz, *An Introduction to Comparative Law*, 3rd ed., Oxford 1998, 63; H.P. Glenn, *Legal Traditions of the World*, Oxford 2000; M.A. Glendon, M. Wallace Gordon & C. Osakwe, *Comparative Legal Traditions*, St Paul, MN 1985; J.H. Merryman, *The Civil Law Tradition*, Stanford, CA 1969. See for a more precise definition of tradition below, Section 1.3.2.

4 Cf. however M. Krygier, 'Law as Tradition', *Law and Philosophy* 5 (1986) 237 and W. Fikentscher, H. Franke & O. Köhler (eds.), *Entstehung und Wandel rechtlicher Traditionen*, München 1980.

field of law.[5] This framework goes to the heart of the study of comparative law in that it seeks to explain differences among existing jurisdictions, albeit from a different perspective than is the case in the present literature.

The argument unfolds in the following way. The starting point is the presumption that legal traditions show essential differences, even though views as to how large these differences actually are may differ. This raises the question of how these differences can be best explained. The three most common explanations are the functionalist approach, the 'culture approach' and the approach cued from differing preferences of citizens. Although all of these approaches have their merits, they only explain pieces of the puzzle rather than the full picture (Section 1.2). Section 1.3 therefore proposes an alternative approach towards explaining differences among jurisdictions, adding an element that has been missing in the discussion until now. Section 1.4 raises the question of whether this theory can be put to the test.

1.2 Legal Traditions and Their Differences

In the standard literature on comparative law, the starting point usually is that existing jurisdictions differ from each other in many different ways. These differences can relate to a variety of issues, ranging from the black letter rules, the manner in which these rules are interpreted by the courts, the structure of the legal system, the underlying legal culture, the efficiency of the jurisdiction involved and many other factors considered by comparative lawyers.

Jurisdictions that differ on essential points from others are usually clustered together in legal traditions or families.[6] The best-known distinction is probably the one between civil law and common law families, which can be distinguished on the basis of their historical background, their prevailing modes of legal thought, the kind of legal sources they acknowledge and their recognition of special distinctive institutions. The intenseness of these differences is highly debated; while some say that they do not relate to divergences at a *deep* level, others regard both legal traditions as unbridgeable.[7]

5 While in Chapter 2 of this book Darwinian analysis is merely used as a *metaphor* for the evolution of a legal system, this chapter takes up a different point, namely that the law *itself* is to some extent the result of an evolutionary process. See for the distinction between these two types of evolutionary work also E.D. Elliott, 'The Evolutionary Tradition in Jurisprudence', *Columbia Law Review* 85 (1985) 38, at 72.

6 A huge scholarship exists on what forms a legal family and which legal families should be distinguished: see, instead of many, J. Husa, 'Farewell to Functionalism or Methodological Tolerance?', *Rabels Zeitschrift für ausländisches und internationales Privatrecht* 67 (2003) 419.

7 In particular P. Legrand, 'European Legal Systems Are Not Converging', *International and Comparative Law Quarterly* 45 (1996) 52, at 61.

Although the intensity of differences among jurisdictions can be debated to no end, there is no denying that differences do exist. This raises the important question of how they can be accounted for and how the differences can be explained among jurisdictions. The explanation is usually found in three different directions: functionalism, diverging cultures and diverging preferences.[8]

In a functionalist approach, differences among jurisdictions are principally explained by reference to *non-essential* factors. In other words, by focusing on the social functions of legal rules or concepts, differences unrelated to this function are perceived as unimportant. The explanation for the differences can then only be that differences are, if looked at from the viewpoint of the function a rule serves, about irrelevant details. In this view, the presumption not only is that universal problems exist, but also that human behaviour itself has universal features in dealing with these problems. As De Coninck and Du Laing explain:

> [F]unctionalist legal comparatists are prone to argue that practically all existing legal systems are to a great extent comparable with one another, simply because they are forced to solve the same or very similar problems occurring in the daily life of society. This affirmation reflects (...) their underlying belief that at least certain aspects of human behavior and human societies are universal.[9]

The second approach explains differences by pointing out that law is closely tied to culture and, as cultures differ, so do laws. This view emphasizes that law is much more than just rules: the meaning of a rule in a particular cultural and national context can only be established after studying this context. And this context, the legal *mentalité*, differs from one country to another. Probably the best known representative of this view is Pierre Legrand, who claims that differences are unbridgeable in the case of continental civil law and English common law.[10] Epistemologically, the common law reasons inductively with an emphasis on facts and related case law, while in the civil law, systematization would be of crucial importance. Whereas the *civilian* tries to rationalize judgments and statutes into a logical system, the common law lawyer has an aversion to formal rules and makes a conscious choice to drive out and even fight continental civil law influence. This choice would stem from cultural differences: an English child is already a *common-law-lawyer in being*, long before it ever knows it wants to be a lawyer.

---

8 Cf. S. Levmore, 'Rethinking Comparative Law: Variety and Uniformity in Ancient and Modern Tort Law', *Tulane Law Review* 61 (1986) 235.

9 J. De Coninck & B. Du Laing, 'Comparative Law, Behavioural Economics and Contemporary Evolutionary Functionalism', SSRN Working Paper, http://papers.ssrn.com/sol3/papers.cfm?abstract_id=1445287.

10 P. Legrand, *International and Comparative Law Quarterly* 45 (1996) 52, at 61 and P. Legrand, 'Against a European Civil Code', *Modern Law Review* 60 (1997) 44.

The third approach offers yet another explanation for differences among jurisdictions. It takes its cue from the idea that different citizens have diverging preferences. These preferences have manifested themselves in decision-making procedures at (usually) the national level, often leading to divergent laws.[11] This does not exclude the possibility that these preferences themselves are also driven by other factors such as the general or economic environment in which the rules function,[12] but in the end they are based on (more or less) rational preferences of people.

Although these three approaches all have their merits, they only explain parts of the puzzle as to why legal traditions differ (or not). In functionalism, it is difficult to account for real 'deep level' differences among jurisdictions, whereas the cultural approach seems to offer a solution for *all* differences in the sense that 'culture' is a black box without much explanatory potential. Finally, the preferences approach does not explain why preferences differ in themselves. In addition, all three approaches fail to make clear why legal systems show a continuous development (can be considered a 'tradition') and thus *continue* to differ from each other on essential points (though perhaps converging on others).

1.3 Legal Traditions and Evolution: Law as a Parasite

In this section, I propose an alternative approach to explaining differences among jurisdictions. This approach is based on the evolutionary framework of memetics and starts with the claim that the main reason why certain legal norms endure in a certain community lies not in (national) culture or in diverging preferences, but in the simple fact that legal norms are replicating entities. To elaborate, what is considered fair in a society is often the result of following the norms that were, coincidentally or not,[13] adopted in the past. What we regard as morally just does not *lead* to certain rules, but it is the *result* of certain rules being followed. This means that jurisdictions may differ from each other simply because they adopted diverging rules in the past and have continued to follow these rules over time. In order to make this point clearer, I will first sketch the theoretical framework this approach is based on and explain an important application in the field of language (Section 1.3.1). From there, I will continue with applying this idea to the divergent development of legal systems (Section 1.3.2).

11 C. Tiebout, 'A Pure Theory of Local Expenditures', *Journal of Political Economy* 64 (1956) 416. Also see A. Ogus, 'Competition Between National Legal Systems: A Contribution of Economic Analysis to Comparative Law', *International and Comparative Law Quarterly* 48 (1999) 405 and G. Wagner, 'The Virtues of Diversity in European Private Law', in Jan Smits (ed.), *The Need for a European Contract Law: Empirical and Legal Perspectives*, Groningen 2005, 5.

12 For a highly contested account of the background of common law and civil law rules see E.L. Glaeser & A. Shleifer, 'Legal Origins', *Quarterly Journal of Economics* 117 (2002) 1193.

13 On this important point, see Section 1.3.2.

1.3.1 A Memetic Theory of Language Evolution: Language as a Parasite

Memetic theories find their origins in the work of Richard Dawkins, who first developed the term *memes* as an analogy to genes in order to describe how Darwinian principles can not only explain the selection of genes, but how they can also explain the spread of ideas and culture.[14] A meme would thus be a self-replicating unit of cultural information (such as tunes, ideas, fashions and catchphrases) that is transmitted from one mind to another. An essential part of this theory is that memes make use of human beings as their hosts to spread themselves. Natural selection explains why some units of information end up being memes and others do not: only certain ideas or cultural habits are favoured in the struggle for selection.

Memetics has received a lot of attention in the last 30 years and has been applied to various academic fields.[15] This chapter focuses on one important application in the field of linguistics, where Frederik Kortlandt and George van Driem developed a theory of language evolution based directly on memetics.[16] This theory regards language not as a human organ or an instinct (as some do), but as a symbiotic organism. In this 'symbiotic theory of language' evolution, it is claimed that over the last two and half million years, humans have developed a genetic predisposition to serve as a host for language as a symbiont or, to put it in more imaginative language, a *parasite*. In other words, language has nestled itself in the human brain after the brain gradually started to become bigger with the emergence of, first, *homo habilis* and, later, *homo sapiens*. Once language had thus 'colonized' the brain, a process of co-evolution[17] of the brain and language started to emerge, with the two reinforcing each other. By the time *homo sapiens* had evolved (about 100,000 years ago), it was a speaking person that moved out of Africa[18] to colonize Eurasia. As Van Driem notes: "Language has enabled man's conquest of the globe (...). Our brain is selectively pre-adapted for

14 See in general R. Dawkins, *The Selfish Gene*, Oxford 1976; O.R. Goodenough, 'Mind Viruses: Culture, Evolution and the Puzzle of Altruism', *Social Science Information* 34 (1995) 287; D.C. Dennett, *Darwin's Dangerous Idea*, Harmondsworth 1995; S. Blackmore, *The Meme Machine*, Oxford 1999; and, applied to law, e.g. S. Deakin, 'Evolution for Our Time: A Theory of Legal Memetics', *Current Legal Problems* 55 (2003) 1.

15 See R. Aunger, *Darwinizing Culture: The Status of Memetics as a Science*, Oxford 2000.

16 F. Kortlandt, 'A Parasitological View of Non-Constructible Sets', in U. Pieper & G. Stickel (eds.), *Studia linguistica diachronica et synchronica* (Festschrift Winter), Berlin 1985, 477; F. Kortlandt, 'The Origin and Nature of the Linguistic Parasite', in B. Bauer & G.-J. Pinault (eds.), *Language in Time and Space* (Festschrift Winter), Berlin 2004, 241; G. Van Driem, *Languages of the Himalayas: An Ethnolinguistic Handbook of the Greater Himalayan Region, containing a Symbiotic Theory of Language*, vol. 1, Leiden 2001.

17 See on co-evolution of genetic and cultural inheritance systems in general the 'dual inheritance theory': R. Boyd & P. J. Richerson, *Culture and the Evolutionary Process*, Chicago 1985 and on the relationship between evolution and culture J.H. Barkow, L. Cosmides & J. Tooby (eds.), *The Adapted Mind: Evolutionary Psychology and the Generation of Culture*. New York 1995.

18 See on the 'out-of-Africa' hypothesis e.g. C. Stringer & P. Andrews, *The Complete World of Human Evolution*, London 2005.

language."[19] So even though bonobos and chimpanzees also have the physical capabilities to speak, they do not do so because of the size of their brain.

It is clear that this is only one specific view of how language originated. Although there is common ground that language must have developed gradually, views differ as to what is its exact origin and how its development took place. One particular view is to look at language as an innate capacity of human beings.[20] Another view considers language to have evolved to enable gossip as a way of social grooming.[21] In the memetic theory of language evolution as proposed by Kortlandt and Van Driem, however, language developed because it was able to nestle itself in the brain and then spread itself by the importance of *meaning.* A critical first step was imitation of words uttered by others.[22] As soon as such imitation occurred, a replicator (meme) was born and spoken language resulted from the success of imitable sounds.[23] But this was no spontaneous process of simple imitation; what is essential is the meaning given to these sounds, for sounds in and of themselves are merely vibrations in the air. In accordance with this view, the first meaning given to a word is seen as the first meme, leading to 'communities of semantic non-constructible sets' that became the first rudimentary languages.[24] As Van Driem explains, "memes need company, and in parasitological terms language requires a community of human hosts."[25] Thus, "language is an organism in the shape of a complex and systematic matrix of grammatical and lexical memes which serves as the vehicle for meme replication in hominid brains." If language is thus seen as a memetic organism (or, in less positive wording, a parasite), it enhances the overall reproductive fitness of its host. If people follow the meanings attached to signs by others (*i.e.*, use language), they are more likely to survive. This explains not only why languages differ, but also why they *continue* to differ among separate communities.

1.3.2 Is Law a Parasite?

Is this particular memetic theory of language evolution also an attractive model to explain differences among jurisdictions? It is well known that imitation plays an important role in the legal field. Following Alan Watson, Gunther Teubner explains that "the legal profession prefers to imitate and take over rules and principles from

19 Van Driem, *Languages of the Himalayas*, 2001, 18.
20 Cf. S. Pinker, *The Language Instinct*, New York 1994.
21 R. Dunbar, *Grooming, Gossip, and the Evolution of Language*, Cambridge, MA 1996.
22 On the idea of language not being an innate capacity, but something one learns through imitation: M. Tomasello, *Constructing a Language: A Usage Based Theory of Language Acquisition*, Cambridge, MA 2003.
23 Van Driem, *Languages of the Himalayas*, 2001, 56.
24 Id., 33.
25 Id., 36.

foreign legal orders".[26] But imitation is even more vital *within* an existing (usually national) legal order. Watson traces this to the peculiarities of legal professionals who need to argue from precedent and authority – they would rather derive their solutions from legal traditions than create something new.[27] Thus, it seems that the law is permeated with "normative self-reference and recursivity and thus creates a preference for internal transfer within the (...) legal system as opposed to the difficult new invention of legal rules out of social issues".[28] In this sense, law is indeed like language; it makes little sense to create a new language or new words within a language if others would not make use of these innovations.

But the important question in this chapter is whether the development of different jurisdictions, much like the development of different languages, can be explained by reference to the idea of memes nestling themselves in the brain. If we scrutinize the model developed by Kortlandt and Van Driem, it seems that three aspects are vital in addressing this question.

The first factor is tradition as such. I regard tradition as the transfer of information within a community over a substantive period of time.[29] As a part of culture, both law and language form such a body of learned behaviours. In particular, the work of the Dutch sociologist Geert Hofstede demonstrates this aspect of learning.[30] He understands culture to be the collective programming of the mind which distinguishes the members of one group or category of people from another. This does not mean such learning has to take place in a conscious way, but it is clear that it does lead to shared tacit assumptions of a group that are taught to new members of the group as the correct way to perceive, think and feel.[31] There is little doubt that legal rules easily meet this criterion, even though the extent to which one is entrenched in one's own legal culture may be a subject of much debate. Legrand emphasizes that one is, by defining culture as

> the framework of intangibles within which an interpretive community operates, which has normative force for this community (...), and which, over the *longue durée*, determines the identity of a community *as community*.[32]

26 G. Teubner, 'Legal Irritants: Good Faith in British Law or How Unifying Law Ends Up in New Divergences', *Modern Law Review* 61 (1998) 11.
27 Watson, *Legal Transplants*, 1993, 95.
28 Teubner, *Modern Law Review* 61 (1998) 11, at 16.
29 Cf. E. Hobsbawm & T. Ranger, *The Invention of Tradition*, Cambridge 1983, 1 who define tradition as 'a set of practices, which seek to inculcate certain values and norms of behaviour by repetition, which automatically implies continuity with the past.'
30 G. Hofstede, *Culture's Consequences*, 2nd ed., Thousand Oaks, CA 2001, 5.
31 For this definition: E.H. Schein, *The Corporate Survival Guide*, San Francisco, CA 2009.
32 P. Legrand, *Fragments on Law-as-Culture*, Deventer 1999, 27. Cf. J.H. Merryman & D.S. Clark, *Comparative Law*, Charlottesville, VA 1978, 29 who refer to 'those historically conditioned, deeply rooted attitudes about the nature of law and about the proper structure and operation of a legal system.'

Others emphasize that one is able to escape one's own culture.[33]

The second essential aspect is to consider that what is transferred from one person to another is *meaning*. As culture is about attaching meaning to facts and behaviour,[34] both language and law are systems of meaning. Clifford Geertz thus rightly sees man as an animal suspended in the web of significance he himself has spun; humans can assign arbitrary meaning to any objects and behaviour. The fact that these meanings are transferred to others and across generations makes both language and law persistent entities that continue to exist even after the people who gave these meanings perish.[35]

The final and most distinctive aspect of the theory is that, as with language, following the law (or rather a particular legal tradition) enhances the reproductive fitness of humans. This may not be the case in standard memetic theory, but adapting the theory of Kortlandt and Van Driem for the development of law implies that the primary reason why certain legal norms endure in a community lies in the fact that these norms are followed regardless of whether they are 'morally correct' from some external viewpoint. It is exactly this point that offers an alternative explanation of comparative variation; regardless of how certain norms have come about (and it may well be that diverging preferences play a role here, next to different cultures and coincidence), the reason why these norms are followed over time is that this enhances people's reproductive fitness.

This idea is not new as such. As far back as 1919,[36] Keller mentioned the idea that following societal rules often gave people a better chance to survive, suggesting that 'law is evolutionary'.[37] He claimed that cultural mores are products of evolution or, more specifically, those "elements common to all codes of laws, over all earthy space and (...) time" would be evolutionary products. They survived because "they respond to a perennial necessity for the very self-preservation of society".[38] The prohibition of murder[39] and stealing would be examples of laws which have such an 'external survival value' in them. After Keller, Jack Hirshleifer also took up this point

33 See on this debate Smits, J.M. Smits, 'Legal Culture as Mental Software, or: How to Overcome National Legal Culture?', in T. Wilhelmsson, E. Paunio, & A. Pohjolainen (eds.), *Private Law and the Many Cultures of Europe*, The Hague 2007, 141.

34 On culture as a system of meaning: C. Geertz, *The Interpretation of Cultures*, New York 1973. There is a close link with so called 'legal significs' on which G.C.J.J. Van den Bergh, 'Jacob Israel de Haan's Legal Significs', *International Journal for the Semiotics of Law* 9 (1996) 81.

35 Cf. J.H. Bodley, *Cultural Anthropology: Tribes, States, and the Global System*, Mountain View, CA 1994.

36 A.G. Keller, 'Law in Evolution', *Yale Law Journal* 28 (1919) 769. But compare already F. Nietzsche, *Die fröhliche Wissenschaft* (1882), Frankfurt am Main 2000, no. 116.

37 His views are discussed by Elliott, *Columbia Law Review* 85 (1985) 38, at 72.

38 Keller, *Yale Law Journal* 28 (1919) 769, at 783.

39 See J. Mikhail, 'Is the Prohibition of Homicide Universal? Evidence from Comparative Criminal Law', *Brooklyn Law Review* 75 (2009) 497.

in a discussion about the efficiency of the common law.[40] He maintains that the very existence of law (and government), hence a shared view of what is appropriate, limits internal fighting and consequent losses of strength for the group as a whole. Thus, if law reduces internal conflict, it gives certain groups an advantage in the struggle to survive.[41] Richard Epstein claims that natural selection works in favour of people with "tastes for legal rules": people that follow certain rules are more likely to survive, implicating that over time, most human beings share norms as "common instinctive responses".[42] Similar views were defended by others.[43]

Interestingly, all of these views claim that, in particular (if not exclusively), rules that are 'common to all codes of laws' (as Keller put it) are the result of an evolutionary process. This becomes very clear in the view defended by the Dutch author Nikolas Roos, who relates the evolutionary nature of law directly to H.L.A. Hart's minimum content of natural law.[44] However, this seems to be an overly limited application of evolutionary theory; viewed in this way, the theory cannot explain why laws *differ*, only why they converge. If law, like language, was able to nestle itself in the human brain as a result of replicating memes, it would be much more likely that different communities have different laws. Indeed, just as languages developed separately, jurisdictions must also show differences because of their separate development over time. Any insightful evolutionary approach to law should be able to explain these differences; as long as different norm-generating communities exist, it is likely that comparative variation is the result of this.

40 J. Hirshleifer, 'Natural Economy versus Political Economy', *Journal of Social and Biological Structures* 1 (1978) 319; J. Hirshleifer, 'Privacy: Its Origin, Function and Future', *Journal of Legal Studies* 9 (1980) 649.

41 R. Epstein, 'A Taste for Privacy?: Evolution and the Emergence of a Naturalistic Ethic', *Journal of Legal Studies* 9 (1980) 665, 670. See Elliott, *Columbia Law Review* 85 (1985) 38, at 77, on which this overview is largely based.

42 See the discussion by Elliott, *Columbia Law Review* 85 (1985) 38, at 82.

43 See notably (in Dutch) H.F.M. Crombag, *Een manier van overleven: psychologische grondslagen van moraal en recht*, Zwolle 1983; N.H.M. Roos, 'Law as a Way to Survive', in P.J. Van Koppen & N.H.M. Roos (eds.), *Rationality, Information and Progress in Psychology and Law*, Maastricht 2000, 239-258 and (in Dutch) L. Logister, *Creatieve democratie: John Dewey's pragmatisme als grondslag voor een democratische samenleving*, Budel 2004, 179: 'Na verloop van tijd zijn (…) morele normen zo geworteld in het alledaagse denken dat hun neiging tot zelfbehoud blijft voortbestaan na het wegvallen van de eraan ten grondslag liggende *habits*.' Cf. W.M. Gordon, 'Legal Tradition, with Particular Reference to Roman Law', in William M. Gordon (ed.), *Roman Law, Scots Law and Legal History: Selected Essays*, Edinburgh 2007, 371: 'Following existing practices may be more likely to gain the necessary approval.'

44 H.L.A. Hart, *The Concept of Law*, Oxford 1961, 193.

1.4 Can We Prove This Memetic Theory of Legal Evolution?

It is now apparent that the specific theory of memetics discussed above may provide an attractive theory to explain not only differences among languages, but also among various jurisdictions. The core of the theory is that law differs because rules came about in communities and following these rules (or rather the meaning they received within that community) enhanced the chance of survival of both individuals within the group and of the group as a whole. Biologically, this process took place because meanings replicated themselves by nestling in the human brain.

This theory provides a much-needed complement to existing explanations on differences among jurisdictions. As we saw in Section 1.2, the prevailing theories only explain a part of the puzzle as to why legal traditions differ: 'law as culture' and 'law as preferences' do offer meaningful explanations of how different laws start out to differ, but they cannot explain why laws continue to differ from each other. In other words, the empirical finding that similar laws of one norm-generating community are transferred from one generation to another (in brief, make up a 'tradition') is difficult to account for in these theories. Looking at law as a parasite explains this in a better way.

The interesting question now is whether we are able to prove this theory in any way. If we leave aside the (unproven) view that the foundations of morality lie in our genes,[45] evidence for a memetic theory of law could be found in two directions. The first is the circumstantial evidence that not only humans but also bonobos and chimpanzees only seem to become moral creatures by learning in a social setting, even though apes are not able to discuss rules of moral conduct as they lack the language skills to do so.[46] This is true even though bonobos that receive language training from their birth are better able to learn language than adult species. On the other hand, humans that are isolated since birth acquire only limited language aptitude and have deficient cognition.[47]

The second strand of evidence is potentially more convincing and directly informed by comparative variation. If law has come about in a similar process as language, we can learn from linguists how they explain differences and similarities among languages. Linguists look at such similarities as signs of contact among

45 See on the idea of genes for morality S. Pinker, 'The Moral Instinct', *The New York Times Magazine* 2008, www.nytimes.com/2008/01/13/magazine/13Psychology-t.html.

46 F. de Waal, *Good Natured: The Origins of Right and Wrong in Humans and Other Animals*, Cambridge MA 1996, 36: "Possibly we are born, not with any specific social norms, but with a learning agenda that tells us which information to imbibe and how to organize it. We could then figure out, understand, and eventually internalize the moral fabric of our native society. Because a similar learning agenda seems to regulate language acquisition, I will speak of *moral ability* as a parallel to language ability. In a sense, we are imprinted upon a particular moral system (…)."

47 Van Driem, *Languages of the Himalayas*, 2001, 64.

communities.[48] In particular, the heartland of Eurasia would have been an area many people passed through, leading to intensive borrowing of 'lexical and grammatical features' and thus to similarities among languages.[49] This view is not uncommon to legal historians who have, time and again, also tried to explain common features in the law by contact among communities. It can be argued that the reason why contract law, as opposed to property law or family law, is largely uniform throughout the world has to do with the very nature of contracting, which allows exchange of goods among individuals even if they come from different communities. Yet another polemic claim by the Dutch jurist E.M. Meijers is that the pre-codification law of inheritance of several European territories was similar because of people migrating from one place to another, taking their laws with them.[50] In his view, this led to the survival of a specific type of inheritance law that was to be found in places as far apart as Liguria, Basque Country, Valais, Corsica and parts of the Netherlands. This type of historical research can help to explain why similarities and differences among jurisdictions exist.[51]

It is clear that conclusive evidence for the memetic theory of legal evolution cannot be provided. But this theory does offer a feasible alternative to other, equally 'unproven', theories about law. It explains why differences among jurisdictions exist by considering legal rules as vehicles for the reproduction of meaning. This view leads away from functionalism (in which legal rules are seen as instruments) and formalism (that exclusively focuses on the structure of rules).[52] It thus eschews the idea that there is a universal morality or universal law that is independent from the community it is a part of.[53]

48 The main goal of Indo-European linguistics is to reconstruct the common ancestor ('Proto-Indo-European') of at present divergent, but related, languages. Cf. B.W. Fortson, *Indo-European Languages and Culture: An Introduction*, 2nd ed., Malden, MA 2010, 3. Meijers (see below) qualifies this as 'legal-geographical research.'

49 Van Driem, *Languages of the Himalayas*, 2001, 64.

50 E.M. Meijers, 'Le droit ligurien de succession', *Tijdschrift voor Rechtsgeschiedenis* 5 (1924) 1, on which (in Dutch) S. Dusil, *Eduard Maurits Meijers en het Ligurische erfrecht in Europa*, Antwerpen-Cambridge 2018.

51 A problem in this respect is that codified laws are often the result of legal reform and not of 'untouched ancient practice': see Fortson, *Indo-European Languages and Culture*, 2010, 24.

52 Here, an interesting parallel can be drawn between the study of law and of language. Legal functionalism finds a parallel in European structuralism (as pioneered by De Saussure) as both see the object of their study (law and language respectively) as an instrument (namely of communication and of reaching an outside goal). Formalism focuses on abstract structures, seeking to create a self-contained and self-referential system in law and a universal (generative) grammar in linguistics, making it possible to predict whether a sentence is grammatically correct or not (as in the work of Chomsky).

53 See for a debate on the existence of a universal morality Pinker, *The New York Times Magazine* 2008. For experimental evidence on the absence of uniform behaviour, see J. Henrich, 'Does Culture Matter in Economic Behavior?', *American Economic Review* 90 (2000) 973.

2 Darwin at Work: How to Explain Legal Change in Transnational and European Private Law?*

2.1 Introduction

This chapter aims to apply some insights from evolutionary theory to transnational private law and in particular to the harmonization of private law in the European Union. By doing so, it hopes to provide a fresh perspective to the theoretical underpinning of the development of both transnational commercial law and European private law. For transnational commercial law, it has already been well explained that the transformation of the role of the State led to new forms of governance.[1] If there was previously a State monopoly on providing legal certainty and enforcement mechanisms, today the goods of legal certainty and enforcement are often provided by others rather than the State institutions, particularly in cross-border transactions. In European private law, an organic development – in which the role of the national States is also rather limited – is the most likely way to create a successful unified law.[2] Both developments raise many questions. This chapter only aims at providing a framework to deal with one of these questions: How to explain the evolution of law beyond the State (of which transnational commercial law and European private law are important examples)?[3] If legal development can no longer be explained by positivist or natural law thinking, can evolutionary theory fill the gap?

As there are many varieties of evolutionary theory, it seems first necessary to sketch the specific evolutionary framework on which this chapter is built. Section 2.2 therefore sets out the analytical presuppositions underlying the application of evolutionary ideas to the development of private law. This framework is a relatively simple one, building on the core of Darwin's idea of natural selection. Section 2.3 subsequently goes on to apply the general framework to understand legal change (looking at law as an organism), while Section 2.4 takes the argument one step

* Published in P. Zumbansen & G.-P. Calliess (eds.), *Law, Economics and Evolutionary Theory*, Cheltenham 2011, 322-334.

1 See e.g. G.-P. Calliess, 'Transnational Civil Regimes: Economic Globalization and the Evolution of Commercial Law', in V. Gessner (ed.), *Legal Certainty Beyond the State: Empirical Studies and Theories of Change*, Oxford 2009, 215 and P. Zumbansen, 'Transnational Law', in J. Smits (ed.), *Elgar Encyclopedia of Comparative Law*, Cheltenham 2006, 738.

2 See further Jan M. Smits, *The Making of European Private Law*, Antwerpen-Oxford 2002.

3 See R. Michaels & N. Jansen, 'Private Law Beyond the State? Europeanization, Globalization, Privatization', *American Journal of Comparative Law* 54 (2006) 843.

further by applying some evolutionary lessons to transnational commercial law and European private law. Section 2.4 raises the important question of what we can learn from evolutionary analysis of law, if anything. Section 2.5 draws some conclusions.

2.2 The Theoretical Model: A Darwinian Evolutionary Framework

Despite the many variations in evolutionary thinking,[4] the core of the theory of evolution as developed in Charles Darwin's *On the Origin of Species*[5] is clear enough. It is that change in organisms takes place through natural selection. The individual members of a species organize their lives so as to produce the most surviving offspring and in doing so, they necessarily adapt themselves to changing circumstances.[6] The descent of one or more trees of life thus leads to a diversity of species through speciation, extinction and the evolution of new characteristics within these species. In Darwinism, this process of evolution by natural selection presupposes three requirements.[7] First, there must be variation in species (otherwise some species could not survive better than others); second, the variation must concern variation in fitness (understood as the ability to survive and reproduce, some species being more able to adapt themselves to changing circumstances than others); third, the characteristics constituent for the fitness of the species must be inherited, meaning they must be able to move from one generation to the next. This means that the heritable *favourable* traits become more common in future generations, while the *non-favourable* traits become *less* common, allowing adaptation of the species as such. Only with these three constituents, a 'struggle for life' in the Darwinian sense can originate.[8]

This idea of development being driven by natural (spontaneous) selection is an extremely successful one. Daniel C. Dennett characterizes Darwin's view as the "single best idea anyone has ever had"[9] claiming that evolutionary theory offers the only explanation for structural change, regardless of the discipline involved. The idea was indeed applied to many other disciplines outside of biology, including political

4 Also see P. Kitcher, 'Philosophy of Biology', in F. Jackson & M. Smith (eds.), *The Oxford Handbook of Contemporary Philosophy*, Oxford 2005, 819.

5 C. Darwin, *On the Origin of Species by Means of Natural Selection* (1859).

6 See W.H. Rodgers, 'Law and Biology', in P. Newman (ed.), *The New Palgrave Dictionary of Economics and the Law, Vol. II*, London 1998, 451 and E. Sober, *The Nature of Selection*, Chicago 1984.

7 E. Sober, *Philosophy of Biology*, New York 1993, 9.

8 Sober, *Philosophy of Biology*, 9 and Kitcher, *The Oxford Handbook of Contemporary Philosophy*, 821.

9 D.C. Dennett, *Darwin's Dangerous Idea*, Harmondsworth 1995, 21. Also see E.O. Wilson, *Consilience*, New York 1998, declaring biology to be the mother of all science.

theory,[10] ethics,[11] economics[12] and psychology.[13] Like in the case of 'real' organisms, social systems and the human brain are also then considered to be developing in a spontaneous way. Consequently, their development is made dependent on two different factors. On the one hand, there is the external environment in which the organism has to survive, while on the other hand there are the internal qualities of the organism itself. The latter decide to what extent adaptation to a changing environment is really possible. Put otherwise, evolution is dependent on both nature (in organisms, the genes) and nurture (the environment).

One can argue about the extent to which either nature or nurture is decisive for the development of an organism. Thus, several years ago, the debate about the most important determinant of human behaviour seemed to have been won by the nurture factor. It was in line with the mainstream cultural climate of the 1960s and 1970s that human behaviour would not primarily be dependent on human genes, as this would go against the idea of society being 'made' by human intervention and equal opportunities for everyone. It was more of Jean-Jacques Rousseau's idea of a human being as a *tabula rasa*: man is born noble and subsequently spoiled by his environment. Today, however, nature is recognized to be just as important as nurture in explaining human behaviour.[14] Thus, Steven Pinker explains how the 'blank slaters' based their idea of equal opportunities for everyone on the wrong assumption that all people have the same genes.[15] This is not the place to delve deeply into this debate; it suffices to say that if law is looked at as an organism being steered by spontaneous selection of rules, both the factor of nature (the intrinsic characteristic of the law) and the factor of nurture (the socio-economic and cultural environment in which the law operates) need to be taken into account.

2.3 UNDERSTANDING LEGAL CHANGE: LAW AS AN ORGANISM

If natural selection is indeed the main factor steering the development of organisms, the question is whether the development of law can also be seen as being guided by this evolutionary process. On first sight, this view may seem mistaken as law is usually seen as either given by some authority (like a legislator or a court) or as derived from some transcendental nature (like in natural law thinking). But this argument

10 F.A. Hayek, *Law, Legislation and Liberty*, London 1973-1979.

11 By e.g. E.O. Wilson, *Sociobiology: The New Synthesis*, Cambridge, MA, 1975 and R. Alexander, *The Biology of Moral Systems*, New York 1987.

12 See e.g. G.M. Hodgson, *Economics and Evolution*, Ann Arbor, MI 1993.

13 See e.g. H. Plotkin, *Evolution in Mind: An Introduction to Evolutionary Psychology*, Harmondsworth 1997.

14 See further Wilson, *Sociobiology*, 1975.

15 S. Pinker, *The Blank Slate: The Modern Denial of Human Nature*, New York 2002.

is mistaken; what the evolutionary perspective has to offer is an *external* account of how law develops. It does not inform us about the contents of law, but only explains why the law develops as it does. This evolutionary perspective was already applied in the 19th century by, *inter alia*, Friedrich Von Savigny[16] and Henry Sumner Maine[17] but it gradually disappeared behind a horizon of more positivist and transcendental accounts of legal development.[18] However, as Section 2.4 demonstrates, looking at law as a spontaneous order of which the development is dependent on both external and internal factors can sometimes be surprisingly insightful.

This section looks at the theoretical hurdles to overcome when applying an evolutionary framework to legal change. The three requirements for natural selection (identified in Section 2.2 above) therefore need to be transplanted to the legal domain. Can we do so?

The first requirement for natural selection is variation in species. The equivalent of this requirement in law is the existence of diverse *national* (and sometimes European) legal rules to solve identical problems. In private law, we have various rules on, for example, the bindingness of an offer, on tort liability and on transfer of property. These rules mainly evolved in national (socio-economic and cultural) environments. They sometimes relate to essential differences between jurisdictions that reflect differing views of society (such as differing levels of solidarity, of duties to help others, levels of social security, etc.).

Second, these rules are also likely to vary in fitness. Many of the present-day rules in the various European countries are the result of a long evolution during which these rules were adapted to the environment they had to operate in. According to evolutionary theory, other rules that once existed in these countries must have been eliminated in this process of natural selection and any change of the environment in the future would – again – lead to adaptation of the present rules. Some rules may become extinct while others become more important. Legal history shows telling examples of this process. Thus, the rule on *laesio enormis* and the *numerus clausus* of contracts in Roman law had to go because they no longer fit the economic environment after the Middle Ages. Rules on animal trials were abolished because of new societal insights. The rule that only men could vote for Parliament also had to be replaced because of a changing societal and political environment.

The third requirement for natural selection (the characteristics constituent for the fitness of the species must be inherited) is more problematic in the context of

16 F.C. Von Savigny, *Vom Beruf unsrer Zeit für Gesetzgebung und Rechtswissenschaft* (1814) and *System des heutigen Römischen Rechts, vol. I*, Berlin 1840, 290.

17 H.J. Sumner Maine, *Ancient Law*, London 1861.

18 Leaving aside the relevance of their work today, Cf. E.D. Elliott, 'The Evolutionary Tradition in Jurisprudence', *Columbia Law Review* 85 (1985) 38, at 43: "By modern standards Savigny's work seems hopelessly metaphorical and unscientific." Also see R.C. Clark, 'The Interdisciplinary Study of Legal Evolution', *Yale Law Journal* 90 (1981) 1238.

law. This is because of the simple fact that descendants taking over the genes of their predecessors do not exist. Rules do not procreate in the literal sense of the word. But one can think of an analogy with genes. In evolutionary economics, Nelson and Winter have used *routines* as playing the same role in firms as genes do in organisms.[19] The routines of a firm establish a *stable identity* of the firm that endures over time and – just like genes – programme its behaviour. As long as the routine is profitable, firms stick to it. The same analogy can be used in law. Rules are not just rules; they are *learnt* by students and *applied* in practice. Normally, agents (in our case, the legal actors) will not deviate from these rules because of considerations of legal certainty and equality. In this sense, the practice of application is being transferred from one generation to another. And just like genes in biological organisms, these rules may gradually change under the influence of a changing environment (society).

Applying these general requirements for evolution to the law allows us to see legal change as a process dependent on both the nature (the inherent characteristics) and the nurture (the environment) of the law. The next question is what this means exactly for the development of transnational commercial law and European private law. Can we indeed apply general evolutionary lessons to these areas?

2.4 Evolutionary Lessons for Transnational and European Private Law

The present debate about the development of transnational commercial law and European private law is to a large extent determined by its *normative* character; it usually takes as a starting point that present national rules are not always suited to deal with transnational commercial relationships or with transactions in the European internal market. Subsequently, one goes on to define the desired *substantive* rules that would better reflect the needs of an international market. This is very clear in the present debate about European private law, in which the question about the *need* for a common European law seems to be less important than efforts to draft actual rules.[20] In this view, as in other opinions of how a more uniform European private law should be achieved, diversity of law is often looked at as a coincidence or historical accident. In this respect, these views focus on what is, at the normative level, a *desired* development. But evolutionary theory has the potential to inform us whether establishing uniform law is also *likely* to happen in this way. The present view falls short of how likely it is that unification efforts, both at the European and

19 J.J. Vromen, 'Evolutionary Economics: Precursors, Paradigmatic Propositions, Puzzles and Prospects', in J. Reijnders (ed.), *Economics and Evolution*, Ann Arbor, MI 1997, 45, at 52.

20 As in the DCFR: C. Von Bar & E. Clive (eds.), *Principles, Definitions and Model Rules of European Private Law: Draft Common Frame of Reference (DCFR)*, München 2009.

at the global level, will succeed and, if so, how this unification is likely to take place. In the following sections, three different evolutionary insights are tested on their usefulness for this harmonization debate.

2.4.1 *The Importance of 'Nature': Path Dependence and Legal Change*

The first possible insight is about the importance of nature. The development of any organism is to a large extent governed by its own characteristics and not so much by its environment. This means that organisms are shaped by transformations in the past that are now irreversible. Human beings will never be able to run the hundred meters in three seconds because their legs and lungs were formed in an environment in which it was apparently not so important to be able to run that fast in order to survive. These characteristics are now constraints upon adaptive change[21] or, put otherwise, the future development is affected by the *path* it has traced out in the past. In biology, it was Stephen J. Gould who pointed out that evolution often depends on 'accidents', leading to a so-called eccentric path.[22] In economics, it is well known that the most efficient organizations may not come out on top because of irreversible decisions made in the past.[23]

The importance of path dependence was also recognized for law.[24] Sometimes rules have become extinct in their past environment even though they could still serve a useful purpose today. A good example of this phenomenon is the elimination of mechanisms that decide which promises are binding and which are not. *Causa* and *laesio enormis* served this particular purpose in continental Europe before the great codifications.[25] However, these concepts lost their main function in the 19th century because of their uselessness in a system that placed more emphasis on the intention to create legal relationships and on the absolute bindingness of contracts. It would have been fruitful to have these concepts available at a later stage, when contract law had to find new ways to decide which contracts were binding upon the parties and which were not. But in most European legal systems, courts were not able to refer to these concepts anymore; they now had to use other legal concepts like good faith and the reliance principle to reach desired results in concrete cases.

---

21 J. Hirshleifer, 'Evolutionary Models in Economics and Law', in U. Witt (ed.), *Evolutionary Economics*, Cheltenham 1993, 205.

22 S.J. Gould, *Wonderful Life*, New York 1989.

23 Hodgson, *Economics and Evolution*, 1993, 204.

24 See e.g. M.J. Roe, 'Chaos and Evolution in Law and Economics', *Harvard Law Review* 109 (1996) 643, at 667.

25 On this J. Gordley, *The Philosophical Foundations of Modern Contract Doctrine*, Oxford 1991 and J. Gordley & A.T. Von Mehren, *An Introduction to the Comparative Study of Private* Law, Cambridge 2006, 461 ff.

It seems useful to look at path dependence in somewhat more detail if we want to establish how it influences transnational private law. Mark J. Roe[26] makes an interesting distinction between weak and strong path dependence. Weak path dependence only explains what has survived; it does not signify that the survivor is better than another: "a society chose between two institutions and the choice became embedded, but the chosen institution functions as well as the one discarded would have."[27] A road may be built on either the left bank or the right bank of the river, but the left bank is not in itself any 'better' than the right bank.

In the case of this weak-form path dependence, there are no obstacles for harmonization. The types of rules one would think of as touched by this form are those related to more technical aspects of law. Whether prescription periods or other time-related devices in law are two years, five years or ten years is usually arbitrary. On the other hand, an evolution toward some 'best' rule is not really feasible here either. Courts are usually not willing to reconsider these types of legal norms once they are put into place by the legislator. In this case, harmonization is therefore only possible through the imposition of a rule in a centralist way.

This makes it important to distinguish these more 'technical' rules from other types of rules. Alan Watson seems to attribute a large role to such arbitrary rules:

> The truth of the matter seems to be that many legal rules make little impact on individuals, and that very often it is important that there be a rule; but what rule actually is adopted is of restricted significance for general human happiness.[28]

As far as the substantive parts of contract law, tort law and the law of property are concerned, I would rather not qualify these as examples of weak-form path dependence. I do not endorse the view that the choice of which rule to adopt is insignificant and that any evolution towards 'better' rules (*i.e.*, better suited for their environment than others) is impossible.

This is not to say that path dependence does *not* play a role in traditional private law disciplines. On the contrary, forms other than weak path dependence[29] are certainly present. If we assume that the Europeanization of private law presents a crisis in the evolutionary sense, the path already taken may thus prevent the best possible rules for the new European environment from evolving. Evolution leading to a great amount of uniformity is the least probable where it is only possible to change the present rules at the expense of high cost. This is least in the case of rules that many

26 Roe, *Harvard Law Review* 109 (1996) 646.
27 Id., 647.
28 A. Watson, *Legal Transplants: An Approach to Comparative Law*, Edinburgh 1974, 96.
29 See further Roe, *Harvard Law Review* 109 (1996) 648.

people rely upon; on the other hand, the amount of uniformity to be attained should theoretically be the most in the case of rules that are only of use for parties that set these rules themselves. Gambaro states the following about the law of real property:

> When one considers the nature of various property rights (obligations between neighbours, riparian rights, condominium law, rights of superficies, servitudes, and the like), it becomes rather clear that much property law is deeply rooted in locally developed legal traditions. And, for this reason it is better left to those local legal traditions which for hundreds of years have addressed these issues in the manner most adapted to the locality.[30]

Gambaro is certainly right, but the reason why these rules are looked at as most adapted to the 'locality', has, in my view, more to do with the investments already made in the path of property law and from which it is too costly to deviate, than with 'the nature' of property rights. To change national law in the areas mentioned by Gambaro would mean that third parties' interests have to be reconsidered on a very large scale. The reliance of the parties involved on the existence of 'absolute' rights that have an effect *erga omnes* would be violated if the applicable rules on, for example, the establishment of limited real rights and the registration of these rights would be eliminated or even changed. The taking into account of so many different interests led to delicate static systems of property law with – in most jurisdictions – a *numerus clausus* of limited real rights. Moreover, to get to know the ins and outs of property law in a specific system is far more difficult than to get to know a country's law of contract; the information costs of the former are higher.[31] In this sense, property law is indeed stuck in a 'local equilibrium'. In most parts of property law this does not pose a true problem, as any need to have uniform law is virtually absent. It is a problem, however, where there *is* a need, namely in the field of security interests – here, the *desire* to create uniform law and the present *practice* as it has evolved in the past (adapted as it is to a national system of law) diverge.

This is all different in the case of the law of contract. The parties to a contract would not be truly hampered by a change of the law because of their ability to set the rules for their relationship themselves. The law of contract's dynamic character guarantees the elimination and survival of rules that are respectively the least and the most suited for their new environment. Rubin says:

30 A. Gambaro, 'Perspectives on the Codification of the Law of Property: An Overview', *European Review of Private Law* 5 (1997) 497.

31 Cf. M. Dreher, 'Wettbewerb oder Vereinheitlichung der Rechtsordnungen in Europa?', *Juristenzeitung* 54 (1999) 105, at 109: 'Da Wissen und Kosten eng miteinander verbunden sind, stellt Unwissenheit zumindest vor Informationskosten und begrenzt so auch die Faktormobilität ganz entscheidend.'

> If conditions change (...) and two individuals decide that, for their purposes, behaviour that was attractive in the past has ceased to be useful, they can voluntarily devise a new contract stipulating any behaviour that they wish.[32]

Evidence from both economic analysis of law and comparative law support this evolutionary thesis. Economic analysis of law shows the need for a distinction between default and mandatory rules. This type of analysis makes clear that rules should be mandatory when any other rule that the parties would adopt would be violating third parties' interests. The number of mandatory rules should decrease in a system where alternative means of protection for third parties are available. For example, there would be less mandatory rules in contract law if the tort system protects third parties.[33] It is obvious that property law is much more related to these mandatory rules than contract law. The economic reason for property law having more mandatory rules runs parallel to the evolutionary idea of property law being less able to change when confronted with a changing environment.

Comparative law also provides us with evidence on the evolutionary thesis. Legal transplants in the field of contract law are far greater than in the field of property law. This may be partly due to private international law's *lex rei sitae* (according to which there is no need to incorporate foreign property rights into one's own legal system), but it is certainly also due to the high costs of transplanting from another system, in the case of property law, and the much lower costs, in the case of contract and tort law. In the latter, legal transplants have been vigorous; the relative uniformity already existent in the field of European contract law is undoubtedly caused by these transplants. In particular, English law was to a great extent influenced by the civil law of the 19th century,[34] as continental European law was influenced in the late 20th century by the law of financial transactions on, for example swaps, lease and franchising, coming from the common law world.

The general lesson is that the evolution of legal norms may not under all circumstances lead to an optimal outcome. Whether a national rule will be replaced by a new European or transnational one also depends on whether lawyers and other legal actors are willing to deviate from existing practices.

32 Quoted by B.L. Benson, 'Evolution of Commercial Law', in Newman, P., *The New Palgrave Dictionary of Economics and the Law, Vol. I*, Palgrave Macmillan UK 1998, 90.

33 U. Mattei & F. Cafaggi, 'Comparative Law and Economics', in Newman, P.,*The New Palgrave Dictionary of Economics and the Law, Vol. I*, Palgrave Macmillan UK 1998, 348.

34 See M. Reimann (ed.), *The Reception of Continental Ideas in the Common Law World 1820-1920*, Berlin 1993.

2.4.2 How Law Develops: A Race to the Bottom?

The second evolutionary insight useful to explain legal change is about the way in which evolution takes place. This is usually not through the complete extinction of a species, but through its adaptation. Evolutionists would say the external identity of an organism remains identical while its contents change. This phenomenon is well known in legal development as well. Legal concepts tend to change as do contents, while remaining the same in terminology and outlook. Contract and property today have completely different content compared to contract and property in Roman times or in the 19th century. This 'Funktionswandel' of a rule takes place more frequently than the clear-cut elimination of a rule.

Evolutionary theory also tells us that the direction in which adaptation takes place is usually toward simplicity, in particular, when homogenization of the environment reduces the number of distinct niches available. The movement is toward complexity when there are only a few species that proliferate within a new environment with many unfilled niches.[35] The more homogeneous an environment is, the more homogeneous the organisms are. In the desert, organisms are less complex than in the rainforest. The interesting question is what this means in the context of legal harmonization. If the direction of adaptation is indeed towards simplicity in the case of homogenization of the environment, this is an indication of the direction private law would take in uniform economies (such as that of the European Union). It seems likely that the more homogeneous the economy is, the more uniform the applicable private law will be. This fits in remarkably well with the criticism usually expressed against allowing a spontaneous selection of the proper rules on the market. Critics of jurisdictional competition emphasize this may lead to a 'race to the bottom'.[36] If private actors are free to choose the law applicable to their relationships with others, it is likely they will choose the law of the jurisdiction with the lowest standards (for example, in the case of American company law, the state of Delaware would be such a jurisdiction). The 'home country control principle' subsequently guarantees this low standard to be exported to other jurisdictions. This race to the bottom may thus be said to arise when "in a deregulated internal market, a state unilaterally lowers its social standards in an attempt to attract business from other states".[37]

The concerns usually expressed about this 'race to the bottom' are mostly normative; the possible lowering of standards is usually seen as a negative thing without too much evidence of this actually happening in practice. Evolutionary theory approaches the problem from a different angle – it shows us to what extent a race to

35 Hirshleifer, *Evolutionary Economics*, 1993, 205.

36 See further, J.S. Kraus, 'Legal Design and the Evolution of Commercial Norms', *Journal of Legal Studies* 26 (1997) 377 and C. Barnard, 'Social Dumping and the Race to the Bottom: Some Lessons for the European Union from Delaware', *European Law Review* 25 (2000) 57.

37 Barnard, *European Law Review* 25 (2000) 57.

the bottom will indeed take place in a changing economic environment. Barnard shows there is little evidence so far of this phenomenon in Europe.[38] She identifies six conditions that have to be met if a race to the bottom is to emerge. Among these conditions are a wide choice of different jurisdictions (like more than 50 legal systems in the United States) and full knowledge of each jurisdiction's characteristics. These requirements were not met in Europe, where – until the 1990s – there were only 15 jurisdictions or less and where it was often difficult to obtain the necessary information about the various legal systems in place.

However, from the evolutionary perspective, a race to the bottom is likely to emerge if these two requirements are met. As to the first requirement, the enlargement of the European Union with new member states implied that the differences between the various systems increased. A migration of companies toward jurisdictions with lower standards is then likely to occur, and there is evidence that this is indeed what happened. In order to meet the condition of full knowledge of all European jurisdictions, the study of comparative law has made great achievements in the last decades. The only barrier for a true race to the bottom would be constituted by the minimum standards of law, set by the European Union's directives and regulations. However, the fact that these standards are a barrier to evolution can also be explained by evolutionary theory; the path that has been traced out in the past has – in Europe – been one of not giving economic considerations the upper hand. A social policy was always part of the European venture. In this sense, the investments already made in this policy would be too costly (perhaps not only in a social or cultural sense, but also in a financial sense in that it would entail large costs of changing the present legal position of workers, the unemployed, and so on) to deviate from.

But not all of the present social guarantees in the European legal systems (namely those guaranteeing more than the European minimum standard) will be kept intact. Hayek is right when he stresses that legal rules may have come into being through historical accident, but that natural selection decides which rules are to survive. The natural selection process then chooses between competing groups of humans, letting those groups survive whose cultural norms and rules are more suited to efficiently coordinate social interactions.[39] The European venture of creating a common market then implies that it is the group of those who are best able to operate on that market whose rules will eventually survive.

38 Id., 70.
39 F.A. Hayek, 'Notes on the Evolution of Systems of Rules of Conduct', in id., *Studies in Philosophy, Politics and Economics*, Chicago 1967, 66.

2.4.3 *Extinction or Living Together?*

The third point is about the results of the evolutionary process. Does evolution lead to the survival of one organism only (with extinction of other organisms) or to different organisms living together at the same time? Biology clearly shows that more fit organisms compete with less fit organisms in a constant struggle for survival.[40] This is even the core of biodiversity. If considered from the viewpoint of efficiency or some other external goal, there would be no need for such diversity, but this way of reasoning misses the point entirely. To consider biodiversity from a functional perspective would be absurd. The mere fact of some organisms being more successful than others is not relevant in this context; each organism has its proper place in the environment of which it is a part. Also, from the economic viewpoint, Cooter and Kornhauser have shown that evolution does not necessarily lead to only one surviving efficient rule, but always to some equilibrium of better and worse rules.[41]

Is this evolutionary insight also of importance to understand legal change? I think it is; it can provide a theoretical explanation and justification for legal diversity. The normative arguments in favour of legal diversity are well known.[42] On the one hand, there is the argument of Tiebout[43] that competition of legal systems leads to more preferences being satisfied. If legal actors can leave the jurisdiction they dislike (they can 'vote with their feet'), national governments are stimulated to make their jurisdiction as attractive as possible. The introduction of uniform law would reduce this exit opportunity and lead to less preferences being satisfied. On the other hand, it is often claimed that legal diversity enhances innovation of existing law since it allows jurisdictions to serve as 'experimenting laboratories'.[44]

These two normative arguments for legal diversity can be supplemented with the evolutionary insight that fit and less fit solutions often coexist at the same time. This insight may not only be used to explain present-day legal diversity, but also to *justify* the existence of different rules to deal with similar problems. In the latter meaning, biodiversity sets an example for the legal domain; it warns us about attempts to

40 Elliott, *Columbia Law Review* 85 (1985) 38, at 70.

41 R. Cooter & R. Kornhauser, 'Can Litigation Improve the Law Without the Help of Judges?', *Journal of Legal Studies* 9 (1980) 139.

42 Cf. J.M. Smits, 'European Private Law: A Plea for a Spontaneous Legal Order', in Deirdre M. Curtin et al. (eds.), *European Integration and Law*, Antwerp-Oxford 2006, 55.

43 C. Tiebout, 'A Pure Theory of Local Expenditures', *Journal of Political Economy* 64 (1956) 416. Cf. A. Ogus, 'Competition Between National Legal Systems: A Contribution of Economic Analysis to Comparative Law', *International and Comparative Law Quarterly* 48 (1999) 405.

44 L. Brandeis, in New State Ice Co. v. Liebmann, 285 U.S. 262: "It is one of the happy incidents of the federal system that a single courageous State may, if its citizens choose, serve as a laboratory; and try novel social and economic experiments without risk to the rest of the country." Also see United States v. Lopez, 514 U.S. 549, at 580-581 (Kennedy, J.): If disagreement exists about how best to accomplish a goal, "the States may perform their role as laboratories for experimentation to devise various solutions where the best solution is far from clear."

eliminate legal diversity in a centralist way. Instead of a European legislator identifying one 'best rule', the selection process should be left to practice. The result of this process may be that not one uniform rule emerges in the end, but this is nothing to worry about. It is the logical result of a spontaneous legal order created by natural selection.

2.5 Conclusions

The aim of this chapter was to establish whether evolutionary theory can help to explain the development of transnational commercial law and European private law. Increasing Europeanization and globalization lead away from traditional explanations for legal change founded in positivist and natural law thinking. The above discussion shows that some evolutionary insights can indeed be applied. The necessary prerequisite for this is to consider law as an evolutionary organism and to apply the three requirements for natural selection to legal change. Once this hurdle is taken into account, the three lessons from evolutionary theory can be applied to law.

The first lesson is about the importance of path dependence – just as organisms are shaped by now irreversible transformations in the past, the law is also affected by the path traced out in its previous development. Legal rules are therefore never completely shaped by the needs of their environment, but are also dependent on their own characteristics. This works out in different ways in different areas of the law. It is likely that transnational commercial law and European contract law are the least affected by the factor of nature and therefore the most susceptible to change.

Second, evolutionary insights are useful to explain how legal change takes place. It is usually not through the complete extinction of a species, but through adaptation that change happens. This adaptation is usually towards more simple species if the environment becomes more homogeneous. This insight can be applied to law: legal diversity is likely to decrease in those areas where the environment becomes more uniform. There is little doubt that this is the case in transnational commercial law and European private law. It remains uncertain whether this uniformity will manifest itself as a 'race to the bottom'.

The third lesson is that evolution often leaves diversity in place – several organisms exist at the same time. This insight can be used to explain why different rules exist to deal with similar problems. This is also true at the European or global level; evolutionary theory can explain why competition of legal rules is to be preferred over centralist unification of law. This does not mean that natural selection of rules will always produce optimal outcomes, but this is because evolutionary theory does not say anything about desired law; it only provides a framework for explanation.

3 Do Small Jurisdictions Have a More Complex Law? A Numerical Experiment in Constitutional and Private Law*

3.1 Introduction

This chapter compares the complexity of legal systems and proposes a possible explanation of differences in jurisdictional complexity. In doing so, it explores uncovered territory – while complexity is a central concept in many academic fields, including mathematics, biology and language, it is largely ignored in the field of law. This is unfortunate because insight into the varying degrees of complexity of legal systems can help us to better understand differences among jurisdictions. While the traditional focus of comparative lawyers is on identifying qualitative differences among jurisdictions, quantitative surveys are lagging behind. This is a pity because it means that existing stereotypes about the complexity of legal systems (e.g., that German law is more complex than French law) remain in place. The following therefore offers an analysis of the law's complexity by using the methods of numerical comparative law.[1]

Good reasons exist to measure the complexity of the law. Jurists often assert that some fields of the law are more difficult to understand than others. In the European legal tradition, private law has long been seen as the more difficult field to grasp, while today constitutional law[2] or tax law[3] are often seen as the more complex areas. In so far as entire jurisdictions are involved, comparative lawyers intuitively assume that some legal systems are more difficult than others. One such intuition is that German law is more sophisticated than most other legal systems. In particular, the belief is that the German Civil Code, once heralded as one of the biggest intellectual

* Published in A. Albarian & O. Moréteau (eds.), *Le droit comparé et /Comparative Law and*, Aix-en-Provence 2016, 473-485.

1 See M.M. Siems, 'Numerical Comparative Law: Do We Need Statistical Evidence in Law in Order to Reduce Complexity?', *Cardozo Journal of International and Comparative Law* 13 (2005) 521 and M.M. Siems, *Comparative Law*, Cambridge 2014, 146 ff. Siems rightly argues that comparative law is in need of new methods that help us to better understand comparative variation.

2 This may be dependent on the particular jurisdiction. For example, the constitutional law of Belgium is generally regarded as highly complicated. See e.g. P. Popelier, 'The Need for Sub-national Constitutions in Federal Theory and Practice: The Belgian Case', *Perspectives on Federalism* 4-2 (2012) E-36.

3 A famous example is the legendary S. 509 (a) US Internal Revenue Code that is seen as standing for the complexity of the field as a whole. See Johnson blog, 'The Hardest Sentence in the Tax Code', *The Economist* 20 April 2011.

achievements of mankind,[4] would have led to a highly complex system of principles, concepts and rules tied together in German legal doctrine that would only be understandable after many years of study. The French Civil Code, on the other hand, is said to even be intelligible to laypeople. Similar differences exist in styles of judicial reasoning. For example, comparatists have been eager to demonstrate how the English style of judicial reasoning is much easier to comprehend than the French or German style.[5] However, all of this is based on intuitions, not on thorough analysis. The question is therefore whether these intuitions are in fact true: are some jurisdictions indeed more complex than others?[6] This academic goal to move away from the stereotypes we may have about jurisdictional complexity already justifies more attention for this issue.

Besides this curiosity-driven academic goal, there is also a practical reason to know more about the complexity of legal systems – it can help legislators and policymakers to improve the law, for example, in achieving deregulation. In the last decade we have been witness to a rise of different initiatives to measure the extent to which a jurisdiction is conducive to the interests of business[7] or the rule of law.[8] Many governments show a desire to improve their position in the periodical ranking in which the simplicity or certainty of the legal framework usually plays a decisive role. In addition, it may also be useful for legal practitioners to know which jurisdiction offers the more attractive law. This can, for example, be relevant when making decisions about the applicable law, where it is likely that the simpler and more accessible the law is, the more readily it will be chosen.[9]

The hypothesis I wish to test is whether there is a correlation between the complexity of a legal system and the size of the population for which this legal system exists. We usually assume that a national law is just as easy or difficult, regardless of the size of the jurisdiction. My hypothesis is that smaller jurisdictions usually have a more complex law than bigger jurisdictions. Put differently, it is no coincidence that

---

4 Cf. R. Zimmermann, 'The German Civil Code and the Development of Private Law in Germany', *Oxford University Comparative Law Forum* 2006, 1.

5 Kötz has spoken of an 'oxygen bath' one is submerged in when reading an English decision after having studied a German one: H. Kötz, 'The Role of the Judge in the Court-room: The Common Law and the Civil Law Compared', *Journal of South African Law* (1987) 35, at 42.

6 The experiment carried out in this chapter does not consider the complexity of specific fields of law within one jurisdiction.

7 *Doing Business 2015: Going Beyond Efficiency*, 12th ed., World Bank 2014 (see www.doingbusiness.org), on which K.E. Davis & M.B. Kruse, 'Taking the Measure of Law: The Case of the *Doing Business* Project', *Law & Social Inquiry* 32 (2007) 1095.

8 As in the Rule of Law Index of the World Justice Project (www.worldjusticeproject.org), on which J.C. Botero & A. Ponce, 'Measuring the Rule of Law', *WJP Working Paper* no. 1, 2010.

9 See on this 'law market' through choice of law by commercial parties G. Cuniberti, 'The International Market for Contracts: The Most Attractive Contract Laws', *Northwestern Journal of International Law & Business* 34 (2014) 455 and S. Vogenauer, 'Regulatory Competition through Choice of Contract Law and Choice of Forum in Europe: Theory and Evidence', *European Review of Private Law* 21 (2013) 13.

the United States has a large population, but also one of the shortest constitutions in the world.

The structure of this chapter is as follows. First, complexity is defined, and it is shown how this concept can be operationalized in law. Such a formalization of complexity is to some extent always a random one. However, one of the aims of this chapter is to suggest one method of formalization and invite criticism to develop future work (Section 3.2). Section 3.3 reports about the actual measuring and presents the results. These results are experimental in the sense that they are based on a preliminary measuring method with a limited number of factors and could still be further elaborated. Section 3.4 continues with a search for possible explanations for the results. Section 3.5 concludes the chapter.

3.2 Formalizing Complexity: How to Measure Complexity in Law?

Complexity is a well-researched topic outside of the law. In fields such as biology, physics, mathematics, epidemiology, linguistics, economics and computer science, there is a thriving discussion about how to measure the complexity of a system.[10] A complex system can be defined as "a system in which large networks of components with no central control and simple rules of operation give rise to collective behaviour, sophisticated information processing, and adaptation via learning or evolution".[11] There is little doubt that the law also qualifies as such a complex adaptive system.[12] However, this does not mean that the methods used in other fields to measure complexity are also applicable to this field. The greatest challenge in considering law as a complex system is to find factors that can be used to measure complexity. I use the term complexity therefore only as a technical term that needs to be operationalized.

Previous attempts to measure the complexity of law are scarce and hardly ever undertaken from a comparative perspective.[13] Following Schuck,[14] my operationalization of legal complexity, and thus of the question of whether a legal system is more

10 Cf. D. Larsen-Freeman & L. Cameron, *Complex Systems and Applied Linguistics*, Oxford 2008.

11 M. Mitchell, *Complexity: A Guided Tour*, Oxford 2009. Unfortunately the law is missing in this cross-disciplinary account of the science of complexity.

12 See e.g. J.B. Ruhl, 'Law's Complexity: A Primer', *Georgia State University Law Review* 24 (2008) 885 and B. Holz, 'Chaos Worth Having: Irreducible Complexity and Pragmatic Jurisprudence', *Minnesota Journal of Law, Science & Technology* 8 (2007) 303.

13 S.B. Long & J.A. Swingen, 'An Approach to the Measurement of Tax Law Complexity', *Journal of the American Taxation Association* 8 (1987) 22; M. Heise, 'Criminal Case Complexity: An Empirical Perspective', *Journal of Empirical Legal Studies* 1 (2004) 331; M.J. Bommarito & D.M. Katz, 'A Mathematical Approach to the Study of the United States Code', *Physica A* 389 (2010) 4195.

14 P.H. Schuck, 'Legal Complexity: Some Causes, Consequences, and Cures', *Duke Law Journal* 42 (1992) 1, at 3. My own specification of the factors differs partly from Schuck's.

complex or simpler, is to look at the different factors of density, technicality, institutional differentiation and indeterminacy.

Density is about the volume of rules in a certain field. The more numerous the rules are (or, formulated more abstractly, the more they occupy the relevant policy space[15]), the more complex the jurisdiction is. This means that a jurisdiction or a field with many detailed statutory rules, or a high number of cases, is regarded as more complex. In a field such as computer science this density is easy to measure by establishing the number of bytes a computer programme would need in order to rebuild the system (so-called *Kolmogorov complexity*).[16] We need another quantification in law in reference to legally relevant factors. Factors one can think of are the number of words or provisions in a written constitution,[17] civil code or penal code or in the average judicial decision, the annual number of enacted statutes or judicial decisions, the number of practicing lawyers per capita[18] or the number of law journals published in a given jurisdiction.[19]

Technicality refers to the use of technical terms that require special expertise in order to understand and apply them. The more technical terms a jurisdiction uses, the more complex it is. Such technicality is not only dependent on the use of specialized wording, but can also follow from, for example, the complexity of the legislative technique. Thus, a high number of cross references in a statute will add to its complexity.[20]

Institutional differentiation is about the extent to which a jurisdiction (or a field within a jurisdiction) can be qualified as a multilevel system.[21] The more autonomous decision structures (subsystems), each with their own claim to legitimacy, exist within a jurisdiction, the more complex this jurisdiction is. My presumption therefore is that a federal system of law, or a multilevel system in general, is more complex than a centralized state in which only one lawmaker exists. The acceptance of private

---

15 Id., 3.

16 M. Li & P. Vitányi, *An Introduction to Kolmogorov Complexity and Its Applications*, 2nd ed., Heidelberg 2008.

17 This criterion was used by R. Cooter & T. Ginsburg, 'Leximetrics: Why the Same Laws are Longer in Some Countries than Others', *University of Illinois Law and Economics Working Papers* LE03-012, 2003.

18 Available in the CEPEJ, *Evaluation Report on European Judicial Systems 2012*, www.coe.int/t/dghl/cooperation/cepej/evaluation/2012/Rapport_en.pdf, 308.

19 Interestingly, the number of law journals differs considerably among jurisdictions. In one count Germany has 789 law journals and the UK 194, while Belgium, as a small country, has no less than 226. See C. Von Bar, 'Die Rolle der juristischen Zeitschriftenliteratur bei der Harmonisierung des Privatrechts in Europa', *Juridica International* XVII (2010) 4.

20 Schuck, *Duke Law Journal* 42 (1992) 4 also mentions the US Internal Revenue Code as an example of a highly technical statute.

21 See also Mitchell, *Complexity*, 109-110 on the degree of hierarchy. Cf. Schuck, *Duke Law Journal* 42 (1992) 4 mentioning product safety as a highly diversified field, governed not only by (different parts of) the common law and statute law, but also by regulatory standards given by different government agencies and private organizations.

regulation as a legitimate source in a given field will also add to the law's complexity. This means that, with the rise of multilevel regulation in the last decades,[22] the law has probably also become more complex. This is in particular true for the jurisdictions of the European Union, that are now all based on an intricate mix of national and European law making without always clarity on which rules should prevail.

The fourth and final factor is the indeterminacy of the law. This factor refers to the clarity of the legal system (or a part thereof), and therefore to the legal certainty that the law can in fact create.[23] A legal system is presumed to be more complex if it is more indeterminate. Relevant in this context is, for example, how many open-ended norms a system contains, how flexible courts are in interpreting rules and what the influence of legal doctrine is on practice.[24] Again, we face specific difficulties when actually measuring this indeterminacy in law. In a field such as thermodynamics, indeterminacy is measured in terms of (Shannon) entropy, which is a measure of disorder.[25] It indicates the amount of surprise a message has for the receiver. Although lawyers can easily relate to this because they know that some legal rules (such as those on prescription of claims) offer more certainty than others (such as the general clauses in tort law), it is more difficult to quantify. One way of operationalizing indeterminacy would be to look at the number of specialized courts under the presumption that the more specialized courts exist, the less indeterminate the law is likely to be as specialization leads to more certainty.[26]

It is important to emphasize that these four factors are not the only possible elements of complexity. It is certainly possible to add others. One can also dispute whether these four factors represent complexity in the best possible way. However, the aim of numerical comparative law is to go beyond a purely qualitative evaluation and to use quantitative factors as a proxy for complexity. Seen in this light, the four above-mentioned factors seem acceptable as indicators of complexity.

---

22 On which L. Hooghe & G. Marks, *Multi-Level Governance and European Integration*, Lanham 2001.

23 Cf. Schuck, *Duke Law Journal* 42 (1992) 4: "Indeterminate rules, processes, and institutions are usually open-textured, flexible, multi-factored, and fluid."

24 On this (concluding that doctrine matters in judicial decision making): E.H. Tiller & F.B. Cross, 'What is Legal Doctrine?', *Northwestern University Law Review* 100 (2006) 517, at 527.

25 C.E. Shannon, 'A Mathematical Theory of Communication', *Bell System Technical Journal* 27 (1948) 379.

26 Voigt, however, argues that judicial specialization could also lead to a less coherent legal system: S. Voigt, 'On the Optimal Number of Courts', *International Review of Law and Economics* 32 (2010) 49.

3.3 The Experiment: Coding the Density of a Legal System

The actual experiment that was carried out consists of an analysis of the complexity of 27 European jurisdictions. The analysis is limited in three ways. First, it is confined to the 27 countries that were members of the European Union in 2012, together with some non-European jurisdictions (US and India), that are used to ascertain whether they support the European outcomes. Secondly, for reasons of available time and space, not all four factors are used in the quantification. The main focus is on the factor density, to be supplemented with one item from the other factors. Thirdly, the main object of investigation consists of written constitutions in so far as these exist in the sample of 27 jurisdictions.[27] Constitutions are ideal objects for a quantitative measurement. It would be even better if one could measure the number of statutes issued every year in a certain country, but it is difficult to do this effectively because of differing perceptions of what a statute is. In some countries, administrative regulations are included, while in some others they are not.

The results of the research can only be presented as experimental as a result of these limitations. However, there is no need to consider all factors in order to find evidence for the hypothesis about the correlation between the size of the population and complexity. The only thing needed is evidence that different factors on the scorecard point in the same direction of either more or less complexity of a jurisdiction.

The actual coding[28] could be based on a 'density scorecard' that potentially consists of 11 different items.[29] This contribution focuses on three items only. The first is the number of words in the written constitution.[30] Of the 26 jurisdictions in the sample, Latvia has the least number of words (4400) and Austria the most (38,000). Other countries with a low number of words are Luxembourg (5500) and Denmark (5500), while Portugal (35,300), Cyprus (31,400) and Malta (30,700) rank high. Germany (26,400) has more than twice as many words in its constitution than France (11,700).

---

27 Coding English law is not only difficult as a result of the lack of a written constitution, but also because reliable data on the number of judges are missing: 90% of cases (mostly criminal cases) are dealt with by Magistrates' courts, composed of non-professional judges.

28 See on coding in legal studies in general C. Shapiro, 'Coding Complexity: Bringing Law to the Empirical Analysis of the Supreme Court', *Hastings Law Journal* 60 (2009) 477.

29 These items could be: 1: number of words in written Constitution; 2: number of words in selected civil codes; 3: Flesch reading ease of written constitution; 4: average length of civil court decisions; 5: number of lawyers per 100,000 inhabitants; 6: total number of courts; 7: number of judges per 100,000 inhabitants; 8: appeals rate as percentage of concluded cases; 9: Doing Business property registration rank; 10: number of words of the implementation of a to-be-specified EU Directive.

30 Cooter & Ginsburg, *University of Illinois Law and Economics Working Papers* LE03-012, 9 also counted these for a more limited sample of jurisdictions; although recent data are available on www.comparativeconstitutionsproject.org, a new count based on the English translations of the 26 constitutions was carried out in this project. The underlying data are available in Table 1 (to be consulted at www.dataverse.nl, project 'Coding Legal Complexity', https://dataverse.nl/dataset.xhtml?persistentId=hdl:10411/20493.

Even if these figures would be corrected for the fact that some languages simply need more words than others to describe the same meaning,[31] the ranking stays intact. This is depicted in Figure 3.1, in which also the two international extremes (the US Constitution with only 4300 words and the Constitution of India with 66,700) are represented.

Figure 3.1 Number of words in constitution

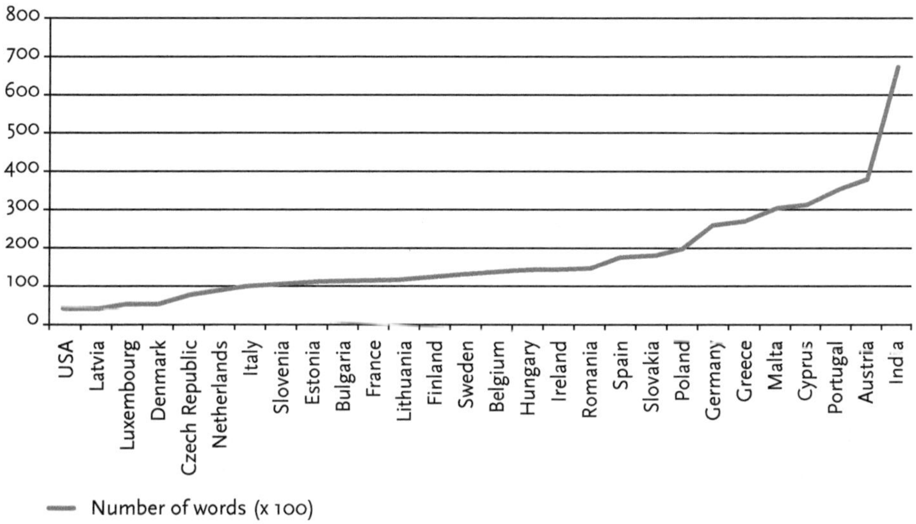

The second item is the so-called Flesch reading ease of the constitution. Flesch reading ease is a readability formula that measures textual difficulty on the basis of the average sentence length and the average number of syllables per word.[32] The lower the score on a scale of 1 to 100, the more difficult it is to read the text. A score of 90 means that the text can be easily understood by an 11-year-old; Time Magazine scores 52. Figure 3.2 demonstrates that the constitutions of Malta (21.2) and Cyprus (23) score very low, meaning that their constitutions are highly difficult to understand, while those of the Netherlands and Luxembourg score best (around 45). The scores of the French (33.1) and German (31.5) constitutions do not substantially differ, but this is different for the civil codes of these two countries. The intuition about the differing complexity of French and German law is confirmed: the German *Bürgerliches Gesetzbuch* (36.9) is almost twice as difficult to read than the French *Code Civil* (61.3), consistent with the different number of words (in English translation, 265,673 words for the German Code and 185,247 words for the French one).

31 On which Cooter & Ginsburg, *University of Illinois Law and Economics Working Papers* LE03-012, 3.
32 R. Flesch, 'A New Readability Yardstick', *Journal of Applied Psychology* 32 (1948) 221.

Figure 3.2 Flesch reading ease of constitution

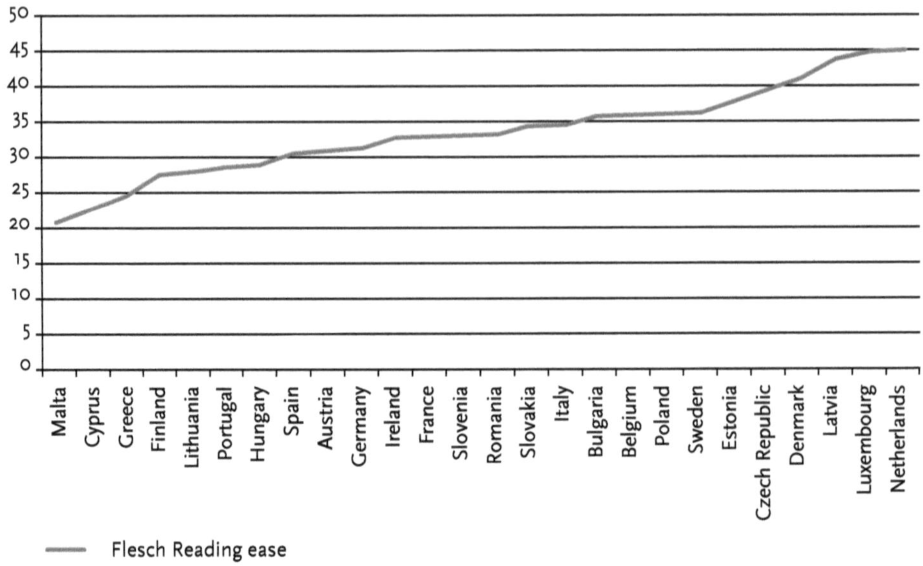

The third measurable item consists of the average length of civil court decisions. Cooter and Ginsburg have shown that this average differs considerably among European jurisdictions.[33] While France has the lowest average number of 548 words, Ireland (4853) and the Netherlands (4016) have the highest numbers (together with the UK, which is not represented in the table). This is depicted in Figure 3.3.

The additional item is taken from the factor indeterminacy of the law and relates to the subjective feelings of citizens on the clarity, publicity, accessibility and stability of law as measured in the World Justice Project on the Rule of Law.[34] This perception of clarity is an essential element of complexity, following the presumption that the more accessible the law is perceived, the less complex it is. Figure 3.4 shows that Romania scores the lowest for this indicator, Sweden the highest.

33 Cooter & Ginsburg, *University of Illinois Law and Economics Working Papers* LE03-012, 9. A brief check on the reliability of these data was carried out by counting the words of 25 randomly selected decisions of 2010 of the French *Cour de Cassation*, the Dutch *Hoge Raad* and the UK Supreme Court. This confirms the data, albeit that the differences are smaller than they were in 2003.

34 See www.worldjusticeproject.org, Rule of Law Index 2014. The data are inserted in Figure 3.4.

Figure 3.3 Average length of civil court decisions in selected jurisdictions (Cooter/Ginsburg)

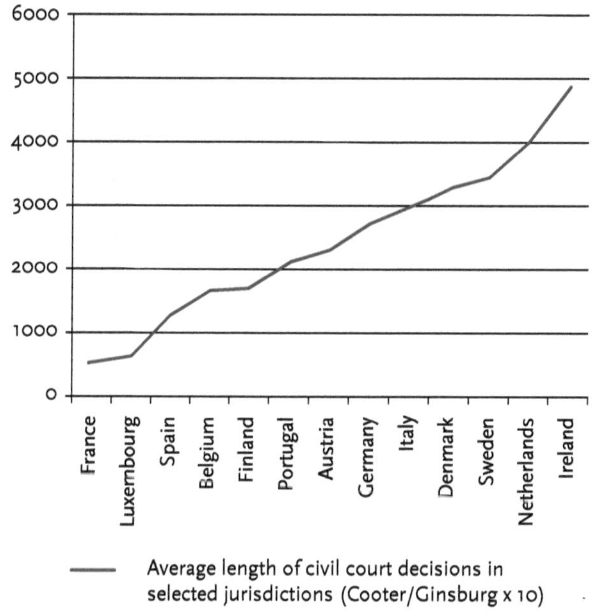

Figure 3.4 Clarity, publicity, accessibility, stability of law (World Justice Project Rule of Law Index)

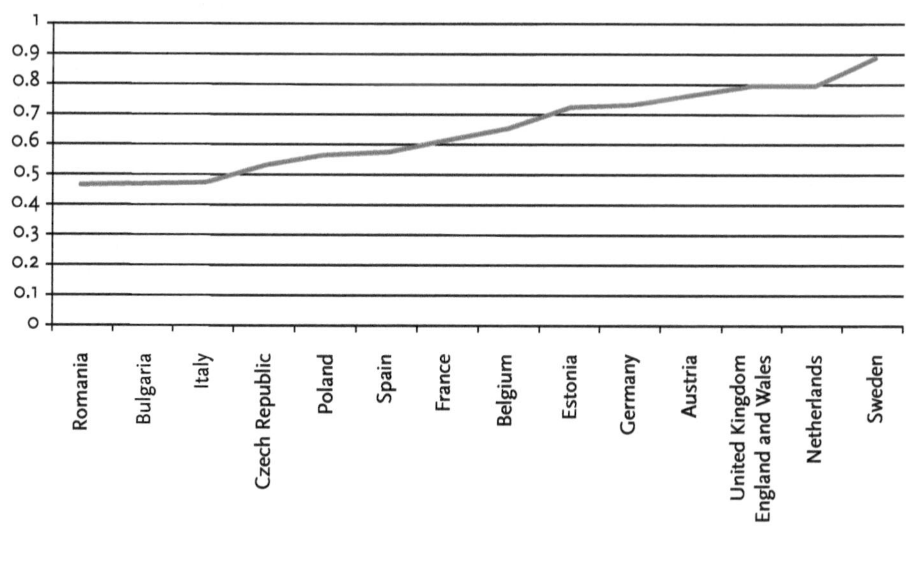

The reason for looking at these four different items is that it only makes sense to speak of less and more complex legal systems if a majority of the measurable items point in the same direction. This in fact appears to be the case – jurisdictions that tend to have many words in their constitution are also inclined to have a low Flesch reading ease and a fairly high average number of words per judicial decision, while its citizens have a less positive perception of the clarity of the law. Thus, Austria and Cyprus tend to score high on complexity, while Denmark, Luxembourg and Latvia score low. However, this is not true on all factors and some jurisdictions are clear outliers. The initial findings suggest that an elaborate statistical analysis of all data would confirm the trend.[35] This merits the conclusion that some jurisdictions are indeed more complex than others.[36]

3.4 Explanation: Why Are Some Jurisdictions More Complex than Others?

If the initial evidence indeed shows that some jurisdictions are more complex than others, the question must be asked how to explain this. If it is assumed that this is not mere coincidence, the explanation could be found in different directions. This is a domain that comparative lawyers do not enter very often; standard comparative law scholarship shies away from looking for causality or correlation between comparative variation and some other factor. In so far as the question is dealt with, comparatists usually refer either to (legal) history[37] or to essential differences in culture or society among different countries.[38] Geert Hofstede provides a more innovative explanation by claiming that countries with a low tolerance for uncertainty (such as Germany) have more specific laws[39] – which makes them more complex. Cooter and Ginsburg on the other hand regard the phenomenon that the same laws are longer in some countries than in others from the viewpoint of agency. Drafters of legislation seek to control the interpretation of the statute by others. The more specific the statute is, the less interpretive discretion exists. They therefore argue that the more the interests of drafters and interpreters diverge, the longer statutory texts will become. For example, if the legislature finds it difficult to pass new legislation (as in Spain), courts have more discretion in interpretation; this has for a result that the Spanish legislature drafts

---

35 Cooter & Ginsburg, *University of Illinois Law and Economics Working Papers* LE03-012, 200310, reach the same conclusion.

36 German law is more complex than French law on the first three items.

37 See e.g. R.C. Van Caenegem, *Judges, Legislators and Professors*, Cambridge 1987.

38 See e.g. resp. P. Legrand, 'European Legal Systems Are Not Converging', *International and Comparative Law Quarterly* 45 (1996) 52 and G. Teubner, 'Legal Irritants: Good Faith in British Law or How Unifying Law Ends Up in New Differences', *Modern Law Review* 61 (1998) 11.

39 G. Hofstede, *Culture's Consequences*, 2nd ed., Thousand Oaks, CA 2001 and www.clearlycultural.com/geert-hofstede-cultural-dimensions/uncertainty-avoidance-index.

longer statutes. If courts apply the law (too) creatively, legislatures then respond with longer statutes to 'punish' them.[40] However, while this explanation may be suited to clarify why statutes are more or less detailed, it cannot explain complexity in the broader sense (consisting of all four factors identified in Section 3.2 above).

This chapter suggests another explanation for differences in jurisdictional complexity. The hypothesis is that a correlation exists between the complexity of a legal system and the size of that jurisdiction's population (meaning the number of people who make use of this jurisdiction) – smaller jurisdictions are more complex than bigger jurisdictions. This hypothesis is stirred by research on linguistics showing that the grammatical complexity of a language correlates negatively with the size of the speech community. In particular, the Finnish linguist Sinnemäki empirically demonstrates that the larger the community of speakers, the simpler the structures of the grammar. It is thus the social environment that shapes the structure of the language.[41] As law and language both share the characteristic of a community of users, the question is justified whether there is a similar correlation in law between complexity and the size of the population.

The hypothesis is tested by relating three of the previously mentioned items of measurement to the size of the population.[42] The first item is the perception of clarity, publicity, accessibility and stability of the law as discussed in Section 3.3. Table 3.1 relates 14 jurisdictions' scores on this item to the size of the population. The results are not entirely conclusive, although it can be seen that the law is perceived as relatively clear (and therefore less complex) in the two biggest jurisdictions, Germany and the United Kingdom, while Bulgaria also fits the hypothesis. Estonia and Italy are clear outliers – Estonia should have had a more complex law, while Italy should have had a more accessible, and therefore less complex, legal system to support the claim this chapter makes.[43]

40 Cooter & Ginsburg, *University of Illinois Law and Economics Working Papers* LE03-012, 12 ff.

41 K. Sinnemäki, 'Complexity in Core Argument Marking and Population Size', in G. Sampson et al. (eds.), *Language Complexity as an Evolving Variable*, Oxford 2009, 126 and id., *Language Universals and Linguistic Complexity*, PhD University of Helsinki 2011. A classic in linguistics is the question to what extent languages are equally complex. See e.g. N. Evans, *Dying Words: Endangered Languages and What They Have to Tell Us*, New York 2009.

42 Figure 3.1 provides the size of the population in 2012 for each of the 27 jurisdictions in the sample. The five biggest jurisdictions are Germany, the UK, France, Italy and Spain, and the five smallest are Luxembourg, Cyprus, Estonia, Slovenia and Latvia. Cf. *United Nations Demographic Yearbook 2012*, United Nations 2013.

43 On a global scale, the United States also fit the hypothesis, with a large population and a high accessibility of 0.72.

Table 3.1 Perception of accessibility and size of population

Country	Total population (2012)	Perception of accessibility
Bulgaria	7,364,570	0.46
Romania	21,680,974	0.46
Italy	57,110,144	0.47
Czechia	10,436,560	0.53
Poland	38,512,000	0.56
Spain	46,815,916	0.57
France	61,399,541	0.61
Belgium	10,296,350	0.65
Estonia	1,294,455	0.72
Germany	82,491,000	0.73
Austria	8,032,926	0.76
Netherlands	16,105,285	0.79
United Kingdom	63,182,000	0.79
Sweden	8,975,670	0.88

Secondly, Table 3.2 shows the relationship between the Flesch reading ease of a country's constitution and the size of the population. The data fit the hypothesis in the sense that the five jurisdictions with the highest reading ease (42.9 on average: Netherlands, Luxembourg, Latvia, Denmark and Czechia) represent together a total population of 34,200,000, while the five jurisdictions with the lowest reading ease (25 on average) represent a total population of 20,700,000. This seems to merit the conclusion that a smaller population's constitution is more difficult to read. However, these are only the data for the five countries at the top and the bottom of the table. The overall picture seems more varied.

Table 3.2 Flesch reading ease and size of population

Country	Total population (2012)	Flesch reading ease
Malta	416,055	21.2
Cyprus	862,000	23
Greece	10,815,197	24.8
Finland	5,375,276	27.8
Lithuania	3,483,972	28.1
Portugal	10,282,306	28.8
Hungary	9,937,628	29
Spain	46,815,916	30.8
Austria	8,032,926	31
Germany	82,491,000	31.5
Ireland	4,588,252	33
France	61,399,541	33.1
Romania	21,680,974	33.4
Slovenia	2,058,051	33.4
Italy	57,110,144	34.7
Slovakia	5,397,036	34.7
Belgium	10,296,350	36
Bulgaria	7,364,570	36
Poland	38,512,000	36
Sweden	8,975,670	36.4
Estonia	1,294,455	37.8
Czechia	10,436,560	39.5
Denmark	5,349,212	41.2
Latvia	2,070,371	43.9
Luxembourg	512,353	44.8
Netherlands	16,105,285	45.1

Table 3.3 reveals how the number of judges per 100,000 inhabitants is related to the size of the population. My presumption is that jurisdictions with more judges are more complex because a higher number of judges probably leads to more diverse outcomes and therefore to a law that is less clear.[44] The average number of judges per

44 More judges could also be the *result* of an unclear law, requiring more judicial decisions. It is irrelevant for my purpose whether a high number of judges is the cause or the result of complexity.

100,000 inhabitants in the sample is 21.[45] The main finding visualized in the table is that the five countries with the smallest population (Malta, Luxembourg, Cyprus, Estonia and Slovenia) have on average 25.2 judges, while the five countries with the highest population apart from the UK[46] (Germany, France, Italy, Spain and Poland) only have 16.8 judges per 100,000 inhabitants. This seems further evidence that bigger countries indeed have a less complex law.

Table 3.3 Number of judges per 100,000 inhabitants and size of population

Country	Total population (2012)	Judges/100,000
Malta	416,055	9
Luxembourg	512,353	40
Cyprus	862,000	12
Estonia	1,294,455	18
Slovenia	2,058,051	47
Latvia	2,070,371	21
Lithuania	3,483,972	26
Ireland	4,588,252	3
Denmark	5,349,212	6
Finland	5,375,276	18
Slovakia	5,397,036	24
Bulgaria	7,364,570	31
Austria	8,032,926	18
Sweden	8,975,670	12
Hungary	9,937,628	28
Portugal	10,282,306	19
Belgium	10,296,350	14
Czechia	10,436,560	29
Greece	10,815,197	23
Netherlands	16,105,285	14
Romania	21,680,974	20
Poland	38,512,000	26
Spain	46,815,916	11
Italy	57,110,144	11
France	61,399,541	11
Germany	82,491,000	25

45 Various comparative statistics exist on the number of judges. See e.g. CEPEJ, *Evaluation Report on European Judicial Systems*, 2012, p. 144.

46 As explained in Section 3.3 above, the table does not include the UK because of a lack of reliable data on the number of judges. However, it is obvious that the UK would fit the hypothesis with few judges for a large population.

The discussion above shows that there is at least preliminary evidence that the thesis about a correlation between complexity and the size of the jurisdiction is correct.[47] The cautious conclusion is that complexity seems to correlate negatively with the size of the jurisdiction. Put more dramatically, there is a reason why the United States has one of the shortest constitutions (4300 words) in the world for a population of 320 million people, while the State of Alabama has one of the longest constitutions (340,000 words) for a population of only 4.5 million. This general trend is not undone by obvious outliers such as India.[48]

If this cautious conclusion is accepted, it begs one final question: is there a plausible reason why a larger country would have a less complex law? One explanation could be that citizens in larger communities have less in common and are therefore in need of a simpler, more transparent, law compared to citizens in smaller jurisdictions. A large jurisdiction simply cannot afford to have a law that is too complex and will therefore tend towards transparency because it must provide the necessary means of living together. In addition, a simpler law is likely to be chosen more often by outsiders,[49] which in turn leads to a larger community of users. The same phenomenon can be seen in linguistics – a large speech community may end up having a language with a less complex grammar because of loose social networks and a great deal of adult language learning by outsiders.[50]

3.5 Conclusions

It is a common assumption that the size of a country's population has nothing to do with the structure of the law. The law of larger jurisdictions is supposedly just as simple or complex as the law of smaller jurisdictions. However, this hypothesis has never been empirically tested. This is surprising in view of the fact that a thriving field of research in linguistics deals with the relationship between language complexity and the size of the speech community. This research shows that grammatical complexity correlates negatively with the size of the speech community: the bigger the community, the simpler the grammar. The aim of this chapter, an experiment in numerical comparative law, was to investigate whether the same is true for the law. The question

47 Data on the ease of contract enforcement (easier in larger jurisdictions because of a presumably clearer law) also provide support – the five best-ranked countries from the sample have, taken together, a higher population than the five that are ranked lowest. See World Bank, *Doing Business 2015*, 90 and www.doingbusiness.org/data/exploretopics/enforcing-contracts.

48 India is supposed to have the longest national constitution in the world for a population of 1.3 billion people.

49 This aspect was not taken into account in the measuring, but it is likely that a less complex law will be chosen more often by foreign parties.

50 Sinnemäki, *Language Universals and Linguistic Complexity*, 64. Cf. Evans, *Dying Words* discussing that in a small speech community many speak their mother tongue, which means that one is able to grasp many more details. A less complex language will attract a greater number of adult second-language learners.

that it sought to answer is whether smaller jurisdictions have a more complex law than bigger jurisdictions and, if so, how this could be explained. The findings, based on the coding of a limited number of factors relevant to complexity, merit the cautious conclusion that there is indeed a correlation between complexity and the size of the jurisdiction. A possible explanation for this is that a large jurisdiction cannot afford to have a law that is too complex and will therefore tend towards transparency in order to provide the necessary means of living together. A smaller community can do with a more complex law because it has a tighter social network. This is something that Aristotle already knew. One can read in his Ethics: "When people are friends, they have no need of justice."[51]

51 Aristotle, *Nicomachean Ethics*, Book VIII, Ch. 1, 120.

4 If You Shoot My Dog, I'ma Kill Yo' Cat: An Enquiry into the Principles of Hip-Hop Law*

4.1 Introduction

There is a growing interest in the relationship between popular music and the law. Building upon the success of the law and literature movement,[1] an increasing number of authors investigate how law and popular culture,[2] including music,[3] interrelate. Articles were already written on references to the law in lyrics by musicians as diverse as Bob Dylan, Tina Turner and Bruce Springsteen.[4] It is in this context surprising that interest in the relationship between hip-hop music and the law is lagging behind.[5] Although hip-hop has become one of the most popular types of popular music, and its lyrics contain frequent references to the law, there has never been a systematic cross-country study of law and hip-hop. This chapter intends to fill this vacuum by offering an inventory and analysis of how the law is perceived in the lyrics of a number of important American and British hip-hop artists.

There are at least three ways in which hip-hop and the law can be related to each other. First, and most important in our view, hip-hop lyrics can inform us about an alternative perception of the law. While official institutions such as legislatures and courts express a mainstream view of the law, hip-hop lyrics convey how the law is understood in an influential subculture. In much the same way as the law and literature movement claims that reading novels can provide us with a narrative that is missed in a traditional account of the law,[6] listening to hip-hop lyrics helps us to

---

* With Andrei Ernst, Steven Iseger and Nida Riaz. Published in *Ars Aequi* 62 (2013) 99-108.

1 For an overview: J. Gaakeer, 'Law and Literature', *IVR Encyclopedia of Jurisprudence, Legal Theory and Philosophy of Law*, www.ivr-enc.info.

2 See A. Chase, 'Toward a Legal Theory of Popular Culture', *Wisconsin Law Review* (1986) 547.

3 J. Jaff, 'Law and Lawyer in Pop Music: A Reason for Self-Reflection', *University of Miami Law Review* 40 (1986) 659; A.B. Long, '[Insert Song Lyrics Here]: The Uses and Misuses of Popular Music Lyrics in Legal Writing', *Washington and Lee Law Review* 64 (2007) 531.

4 See resp. Adam Gearey, 'Outlaw Blues: Law in the Songs of Bob Dylan', *Cardozo Law Review* 20 (1999) 1401; G. Minda, 'Phenomenology, Tina Turner and the Law', *New Mexico Law Review* 16 (1986) 479; A. Smith, 'The Dignity and Humanity of Bruce Springsteen's Criminals', *Widener Law Journal* 14 (2005) 787.

5 See, however, P. Butler, 'Much Respect: Towards a Hip-Hop Theory of Punishment', *Stanford Law Review* 56 (2004) 983, id., *Let's Get Free: A Hip-Hop Theory of Justice*, New York 2010 and the website http://hiphoplaw.blogspot.be. This literature, however, focuses almost entirely on criminal law.

6 See e.g. R. Weisberg, *Poethics: Toward a Literary Jurisprudence*, New York 1992.

understand how law can be seen differently. Thousands of available lyrics inform us about life in the urban ghettos of today and thus provide information about law in a bottom-up way that is otherwise very difficult to access. Put differently, lyrics provide insights that could otherwise only become available through time-consuming sociological or anthropological research.

Second, knowledge about how the law is represented in hip-hop music can be important to understand the behaviour of an individual claimant or defendant. Popular culture, in the form of literature, films, television series and music, affects a layperson's perception of the law. It thus often adds to the emancipation of the layperson's legal mind in a much better way than the official institutions could ever achieve. The general audience is, for example, well aware of the rights it has when being arrested as a result of the many television series and films in which the police officer actually reads the defendant his or her rights. A better understanding of where individuals derive their legal knowledge from – even if based on false information – can be useful to the judiciary when making decisions.

Finally, hip-hop and the law are related when the question needs to be answered whether lyrics can be admitted as criminal evidence.[7] If lyrics are seen as autobiographical, and thus depict real-life events, they can play a role in revealing the criminal intent of the defendant. This use of hip-hop lyrics is commonly accepted in the United States courts. For example, in the case of *United States v. Foster*,[8] the defendant was caught carrying two suitcases full of drugs. The police found a handwritten rap lyric in his bag containing the sentence *Key for Key, Pound for Pound, I'm the biggest Dope Dealer and I serve all over town*. This line was accepted as evidence of the defendant's intention to distribute drugs.[9]

The focus in this chapter is on the first aspect. Our aim is to investigate whether it is possible to find legal principles immanent in hip-hop lyrics. If the creation of a legal system were left to rappers, what would this system look like and in what way would it differ from existing legal systems?[10] We do not assume a coherent and largely uniform view of the law in all varieties of hip-hop produced around the world, but we do

7 On which A. Dennis, 'Poetic (In)Justice? Rap Music Lyrics as Art, Life, and Criminal Evidence', *Columbia Journal of Law and the Arts* 31 (2007) 1.

8 939 F.2nd, 445 (7th Circuit, 1991), at 448-449.

9 A fifth possible relation between law and hip-hop is when courts use lyrics in their decisions, not uncommon in the United States. Long, *Washington and Lee Law Review* 64 (2007), at 540 shows that Bob Dylan is the most cited musician in American court decisions (26 times), followed by Paul Simon and Bruce Springsteen. In particular, Dylan's probably most famous sentence 'The Times They Are A-Changin' was cited more than once in order to illustrate a changed view of what the law should entail. Dylan was also quoted by Supreme Court judges Roberts and Scalia. In the case *Deangelo Bailey v. Eminem*, Michigan Circuit Court judge Deborah Servitto rapped a part of the decision: see http://lawhaha.com/the-real-slim-shady-is-not-a-michigan-trial-judge.

10 In this respect, we follow the path set out by Butler, *Stanford Law Review* 56 (2004), at 1001 ff., who aims to demonstrate how hip-hop informs a principled theory of punishment. Our investigation, however, is broader as we do not limit ourselves to criminal law.

believe that the artists we selected are representative of the hip-hop movement. After an explanation of our methodology (Section 4.2), we proceed with an identification of the principles we were able to identify in the reviewed lyrics (Section 4.3). Section 4.4 concludes the chapter.

4.2 Methodology

Hip-hop music[11] originated in the New York South Bronx in the 1970s and became known internationally through artists like Sugarhill Gang ('Rapper's Delight', 1979), Run-DMC ('Walk this Way', 1986), Salt-N-Pepa ('Push it', 1988) and Public Enemy ('Fight the Power', 1989). While these artists are already widely diverse, hip-hop has diversified even further in the last 20 years. Even within mainstream hip-hop music, various styles were developed (including East Coast and West Coast hip-hop and gangsta rap).[12] Today, hip-hop is usually associated with bestselling American artists like 50 Cent, Eminem and Jay-Z. Adding to the current diversity of different types of hip-hop in the United States are the many national varieties of hip-hop throughout the world. This worldwide expansion turned hip-hop into the second best sold type of popular music. Hip-hop as a social movement and a lifestyle (and not only as a form of music) can be best described as being about resistance against the status quo (including the law).[13] This is already evident from many of the names that hip-hop artists use (such as Public Enemy, Big Punisher, Beastie Boys, Missy 'Misdemeanor' Elliott and OutKast), but it is even more apparent from the controversial lyrics of many hip-hop artists.

The high number of hip-hop artists and their diversity of styles pose a methodological problem. We chose to select the artists for our research on the basis of three criteria: their nationality, their influence and the likelihood of the artist making reference to the law. In terms of nationality, we restricted ourselves to artists from the United States and the United Kingdom in view of the importance of these countries in worldwide hip-hop culture. Within the group of artists from the US and the UK, we measured their influence by asking five students (all well-informed about hip-hop music) to make a list of hip-hoppers they considered the ten most influential 'mainstream' artists. Their lists were checked against the (American) Rolling Stone

11 See J. Chang, *Can't Stop, Won't Stop: A History of the Hip-Hop Generation*, New York 2005.

12 See for an overview based on periods: A. Bradley & A. Dubois (eds.), *The Anthology of Rap*, New Haven, CT 2010. A different type of categorization is offered in the excellent Wikipedia entry on hip-hop music, available at http://en.wikipedia.org/wiki/Hip_hop_music.

13 Cf. N.J. Sciullo, 'Conversations with the Law: Irony, Hyperbole, and Identity Politics or Sake Pase?', *Oklahoma City University LR* 34 (2009) 455.

Magazine 'King of Hip-Hop' election[14] and against various listings in the (British) New Musical Express.[15] This was followed by a random check of the extent to which the selected artists' lyrics were likely to refer to the law.[16] This led to the selection of five US artists and six UK artists whom we believe to be representative of today's mainstream[17] hip-hop in their respective countries. These are Dr. Dre (André Romell Young, born Los Angeles 1965), Jay-Z (Shawn Corey Carter, born New York City 1969), Eminem (Marshall Bruce Mathers III, born Detroit 1972), 50 Cent (Curtis James Jackson III, born New York City 1975), Ludacris (Christopher Brian Bridges, born Champaign 1977), Ms. Dynamite (Niomi Arleen Daley, born London 1981), Professor Green (Stephen Paul Manderson, born London 1983), Dizzee Rascal (Dylan Kwabena Mills, born London 1984), Plan B (Benjamin Paul Drew, born London 1984), Tinie Tempah (Patrick Chukwuem Okogwu Jr., born London 1988) and N-Dubz (a group consisting of Constadinos Contostavlos, born London 1987, Richard Rawson, born London 1987 and Tulisa Contostavlos, born London 1988).

In the next step, we selected the two[18] bestselling albums of each of these artists on the basis of data on the recording industry.[19] Selected were The Marshall Mathers LP (Eminem, 2000), The Eminem Show (Eminem, 2002), Get Rich or Die Tryin' (50 Cent, 2003), The Massacre (50 Cent, 2005), The Chronic (Dr. Dre, 1992), 2001 (Dr. Dre, 1999), Word of Mouf (Ludacris, 2001), Chicken 'N Beer (Ludacris, 2003), Vol. 2 Hard Knock Life (Jay-Z, 1998), The Black Album (Jay-Z, 2003), A Little Deeper (Ms. Dynamite, 2002), Judgement Days (Ms. Dynamite, 2005), Maths + English (Dizzee Rascal, 2007), Tongue 'N Cheek (Dizzee Rascal, 2009), Who Needs Actions When You Got Words (Plan B, 2006), The Defamation of Strickland Banks (Plan B, 2010), Disc-Overy (Tinie Tempah, 2010), Alive Till I'm Dead (Professor Green, 2010),

14 C. Molanphy, 'Introducing the King of Hip-Hop', *Rolling Stone Magazine* 15 August 2011. The election was based on album sales, charts, YouTube views, income from touring, Facebook likes, album reviews and awards. It puts Eminem on 1, Jay-Z on 5 and Ludacris on 8. 50 Cent and Dr. Dre are not on the list.

15 Several lists on www.nme.com were looked at to get an impression of the popularity of the selected artists.

16 This first check was based on the keywords promise, family, authority, government, police, justice, prison, fairness, judges, lawyers, free speech, jail, refugees, drugs and weapons (and their equivalents in slang).

17 We do acknowledge that the image of hip-hop music is also influence stedd by non-mainstream artists such as, in the United States, Blu (Johnson Barnes, born San Pedro, Cal. 1983) and, in the United Kingdom, Kano (Kane Brett Robinson, born London 1985), but did not consider their lyrics for inclusion in the project.

18 UK artist Tinie Tempah released only one album so far, but because of its success it was also included in the sample. In order to reach 20 albums in total, the bestselling album of Professor Green was added to the list.

19 For the US artists, data were retrieved from the Recording Industry Association of America (RIAA), available at www.riaa.com. Data for the UK are available on the website of the British Recorded Music Industry (www.bpi.co.uk). Sales in our sample range from 10.4 million for Eminem's The Marshall Mathers LP to 60,000 for Plan B's Who Needs Actions When You Got Words.

Uncle B (N-Dubz, 2008) and Love Live Life (N-Dubz, 2010). The total of 290 songs on the selected albums formed the basis for our investigation.

One methodological problem deserves separate attention. It is likely that when hip-hop emerged in the 1970s, the lyrics reflected real-life experiences of the artists. This may no longer be true today, even though all five selected American artists have witnessed gang violence and some of them were in fact arrested (with 50 Cent being notorious for having been a crack dealer as a teenager and being shot three times at age 24). Most of the selected British artists grew up on council estates and Professor Green is known to have sold drugs in Hackney, East London, where he grew up. Although it is tempting to find parallels between the artists' lyrics and their personal lives (facilitated by the autobiographies that some of them wrote[20]), we will not attempt to do so. This chapter assumes there is something like a coherent hip-hop lifestyle that is based partly on the experiences of the artists and their relatives and friends, and partly on some idealized hip-hop culture. This idealized 'hip-hop nation' means that the lyrics often refer to role models (such as some idealized picture of a gangster, drug dealer or pimp) and are even ironic.[21] Viewed from our perspective, it does not therefore matter if the lyrics do not (completely) reflect real-life events or real personal emotions of their authors.[22]

4.3 Principles of Hip-Hop Law

4.3.1 *Introduction*

Scrutiny of the 290 songs on the selected albums leads to the identification of four principles of hip-hop law. This does not mean that no other principles exist,[23] but we believe these four are the most important ones. We discuss the principles below. We explicitly choose to incorporate relevant lyrics in the main text. We also refer to lyrics by other hip-hop artists in so far as these are known to us.[24]

20 See Eminem, *The Way I Am*, New York 2008; 50 Cent, *From Pieces to Weight*, New York 2004; Jay-Z, *Decoded*, New York 2011. The British artists also seem to have rapped about their criminal past (see e.g. Dizzee Rascal in 'World Outside' (2007), Professor Green in 'Just be Good to Green' (2010) and N-Dubz in 'Secrets' (2008)).

21 On which Sciullo, *Oklahoma City University LR* 34 (2009), at 481.

22 We made use of the archives of hip-hop lyrics available at e.g. http://ohhla.com/all.html and www.hiphoparchive.org.

23 The lyrics contain regular references to racial discrimination and to freedom of expression. As the hip-hop view on this does not fundamentally differ from the mainstream view, we decided not to pay further attention to these.

24 Other artists than those in our sample of 11 are quoted by the title of the song and the year of release.

4.3.2 Punishment: An Eye for an Eye

It is commonplace to distinguish between several goals of criminal law. Next to retribution, rehabilitation, protection and education of the offender, (specific and general) deterrence, incapacitation and restoration are among the goals that criminal justice systems seek to achieve.[25] Each country tends to prioritize one goal over another, building the criminal justice system that it considers most in line with its own community values.

Our analysis confirms the previous findings of Paul Butler that hip-hop denies any utilitarian goals of punishment.[26] The idea that criminal law should aim for social benefits such as crime reduction is not shared in hip-hop lyrics. Instead, the lyrics suggest that the law does not in any way prevent crime. Jay-Z, who often expresses his view of criminal law and the justice system, is not deterred from crime as he makes clear when he raps: *I probably owe it to y'all, probably to be locked by the force / Tryin' to hustle some things, that go with the Porsche / Feelin' no remorse, feelin' like my hand was forced / Middle finger to the law, (...).*[27] This general insensitivity to the law is also very clear in the lyrics of 50 Cent. In a style that is definitely more aggressive than that of Jay-Z, he makes it clear that the police, the law and possible imprisonment do not deter him from committing crimes. In his song 'Heat' (2003), he states: *I do what I gotta do I don't care if I get caught / The DA can play this motherfuckin' tape in court.* Likewise, hip-hop artists do not seem to believe in the value of restorative justice, such as reintegrating the offender into society. Jay-Z recalls that being sent to prison does not make someone another person because he still has to go back to where he came from: *For 3 years they had me peeing out of a cup / Now they 'bout to free me up what you think I'm gone be, what / Rehabilitated man I still feel hatred.*[28]

This sceptical view of the educating value of criminal justice can be easily explained. The philosophy of hip-hop culture is that people living in socially deprived areas cannot help committing crimes if this is what they see around them all day and if they have no other way to make an income. OutKast narrates: *Knowing each and every nigger sellin', but can you blame/ The fact the only way a brother can survive the game.*[29] This is not any different in Britain; in his song 'World Outside', Dizzee Rascal narrates: *Running around hype and criminal antics fed me for a while / But studio gave me a lot more creative style.* This does not make it right if a poor person sells drugs

---

25 See for a critical reflection upon the goals of criminal law G.P. Fletcher, *Rethinking Criminal Law*, Oxford 2000.

26 Butler, *Stanford Law Review* 56 (2004), at 1001 ff. See also A.D. Pond Cummings, 'Thug Life: Hip Hop's Curious Relationship with Criminal Justice', *Santa Clara Law Review* 50 (2009) 515.

27 'Dirt Off Your Shoulder' (2003). In the song '99 Problems' (2003), Jay-Z remarks: *In my rearview mirror is the motherfucking law.*

28 'Threat' (2003).

29 'Mainstream' (1996), quoted by Butler, *Stanford Law Review* 56 (2004), at 1005.

in order to make an income, but in a hip-hop view of the law it is seen as wrong to punish this person severely.

In addition, one of the most important features of hip-hop lyrics is that the criminal justice system is criticized for being discriminatory against the socially and financially deprived because of the type of conduct that is criminalized. If people feel that prosecution of offenders is based on the wrong criteria, one cannot expect them to show better behaviour after their return from prison. The best-known example of this inequality in the American justice system has long been the Anti-Drug Abuse Act 1986. This statute was meant to fight the use of drugs in inner city neighbourhoods. It put a mandatory minimum sentence of five years on the possession of crack (cocaine mixed with baking soda so that it can be smoked) and an even higher sentence on selling this drug. Users and dealers of powder cocaine received much lower sentences.[30] The result of this was that poor African Americans in inner cities (typically users of the less expensive crack) were prosecuted and sentenced more heavily than users and sellers of regular cocaine. This led to a much criticized 100 to 1 ratio – crack users were likely to be punished 100 times more heavily than powder cocaine users. In 2010, the punishment regime was changed under the new Fair Sentencing Act, which reduced the disparity to 18 to 1. This bias against certain types of drug use, leading the police to act primarily against young Afro-Americans,[31] has not gone unnoticed in hip-hop circles.[32] Already in 1988, KRS-One noted that: *In society we have illegal and legal / We need both, to make things equal / So legal is tobacco, illegal is speed / Legal is aspirin, illegal is weed.*[33] A bias against African Americans is also mentioned in Jay-Z's song '99 Problems' (2003), in which the portrayed young male is pulled over by the police because *he was doing fifty-five in a fifty-four*, a speed zone that does not exist but that can be seen as a hyperbole for being prosecuted for a wrong that was not really committed.

If criminal law does not serve to prevent people from committing crimes and successful reintegration in society is not likely, then what is the goal of punishment in a hip-hop view of the law? It seems that simple retribution is the only true justification for punishing criminals; the justice system is there to offer a proportionate response to the offense.[34] This principle of 'an eye for an eye' can be discerned in many lyrics. One prominent example is in Jay-Z's 'Justify My Thug' (2003): *If you shoot my dog, I'ma kill yo' cat / Just the unwritten laws in rap – know dat / For every action there's*

30 Anti-Drug Abuse Act 1986. See Butler, *Stanford Law Review* 56 (2004), at 988 and D.A. Sklansky, 'Cocaine, Race, and Equal Protection', *Stanford Law Review* 47 (1995) 1283.

31 And also leading to a disparity in prison population; statistics show that 50% of imprisoned men in the United States are African American, while only 12% of the American population is black.

32 Cf. Public Enemy, 'Fight the Power' (1989): *You see one in every 100 Americans are locked up / One in every 9 black Americans are locked up.*

33 'Illegal Business' (1988), quoted by Butler, *Stanford Law Review* 56 (2004), at 1008.

34 See M.J. Fish, 'An Eye for an Eye: Proportionality as a Moral Principle of Punishment', *Oxford Journal of Legal Studies* 28 (2008) 57.

a reaction. Grammy Award winner Nelly also reminds us of this law of biblical and Islamic[35] retaliation: *if you take a life, you gon' lose yours too.*[36] It seems that hip-hop artists eagerly accept it as morally correct that criminal behaviour should be punished with a sentence identical to the offense. A harsh sentence for an offence seen as discriminatory (such as possession of crack) is not regarded as proportionate. This emphasis on retaliation also means that it would be wrong to state that in hip-hop criminal justice is held in low esteem simply because criminals are against any prosecution. Prosecution is needed, albeit for another reason than is accepted in most official jurisdictions.

4.3.3 Self-Justice and Self-Government

A second principle of hip-hop law consists of self-government and the desire to take the law into one's own hands (self-justice). When we discussed the principle of retribution, it was still left open *who* would retaliate – the official State institutions or the victim itself. The lyrics consistently show a preference for the latter; they tend to describe how hip-hop characters counter strike against those who attack them as a form of *street justice*. The aim of this is to get even and ultimately to prevent a person from being victimized again. The reasonable limits of self-defence as defined in national jurisdictions are not respected. Thus, the character portrayed in Dr. Dre's 'Let Me Ride' (1992) arms himself to protect himself against others carrying weapons: *I got my Glock cocked cuz niggaz want these. Now soon as I said it, seems I got sweated / By some nigga with a Tec 9 tryin' to take mine. Ya wanna make noise, make noise.*[37] In the autobiographical song 'Many Men (Wish Death)', 50 Cent relates: *Hommo shot me, three weeks later he got shot down / Now it's clear that I'm here, for a real reason / 'Cause he got hit like I got hit, but he ain't fucking breathing.* The song refers to 50 Cent being shot in May 2000 by Darryl 'Homicide' (or 'Hommo') Baum. Three weeks later three gunmen killed Darryl Baum himself. Ludacris also makes clear what to expect when being harassed: *Just keep on pissin' me off, like a weak kidney / And you will find your family reading your obituary.*[38]

British rappers are eager to confirm the importance of taking the law into one's own hands. When Professor Green raps about life being tough and children living on council estates using weapons from a young age to protect themselves, he states: *It's blitz amidst the strife here, got kids with sticks and knifes here / It's hype here, we know no different prick; it's just life here, life the way we know from young the way we're shown.* Plan B's song 'No Good' (2006) is one long warning not to use violence

35 Exodus 21:23-25 and Qur'an 2:178.
36 'Nellyville' (2002).
37 A Glock is a popular Austrian-made handgun, a Tec-9 a semi-automatic handgun produced by American manufacturer Intratec.
38 'Get the Fuck Back' (2001).

against the main character to avoid any counter violence in return: *Don't fucking cross my line, yo / I'll hit you so hard your arse will hit the floor in Cairo / I know how to take your life and make you die, yo / So watch your fucking step and where you place your fucking eyes bro.* The need for self-protection is also evident from Dr. Dre's song 'Forgot About Dre' (2000). In Compton, Los Angeles (*the home of drive-bys and ak-matics, swap meets, sticky green, and bad traffic*[39]) violent crime occurs more often than in average California. This leaves Dr. Dre reluctant to give up his weapons: *Now you wanna run around and talk about guns, like I ain't got none / What you think I sold 'em all?*

It is obvious that the principle of self-justice follows from the feeling among rappers that the law does not sufficiently protect them. This is not only the case because they feel that the State does not want to protect them in the same way as other people are protected, but also because their aim in life is to become rich at any cost and preferably without being 'harassed' too much by the government or the police; many lyrics narrate how the ultimate goal of drug dealing and committing other crimes is to gain wealth. The title of 50 Cent's album (2003) and film (2005) 'Get Rich Or Die Tryin'' already reveals this desire. There is an inconsistency here with what we previously encountered as a justification for criminal behaviour, namely that it is needed in order to survive.

Hip-hop not only questions the ability of courts to reach fair outcomes in concrete cases, but the criticism of the judiciary and of other official institutions is also a recurrent theme. In 'Fuck Tha Police' (1988), Dr. Dre's former rap group N.W.A. (Niggaz Wit' Attitudes) describes a fictitious case against the police department in an especially designed 'N.W.A. court': *Right about now N.W.A court is in full effect / Judge Dre presiding in the case of N.W.A versus the police department*'. Also, the national parliaments are not seen as representing the interests of the least privileged in society. Eminem, in particular, is known for being outspoken about the failure of democracy. The aim of rapping about the US Congress is *to spit liquor in the faces of this Democracy of Hypocrisy.*[40] Ms. Dynamite directly addresses the British Prime Minister: *How much hundred seats in parliament / It's so unfair but so clear / Don't none of them represent me / And ain't one of them represent my peers / And it don't matter who we vote for, nor who gets in / The poor keep dying and the rich keep living / Mothers keep losing their children to the system / They stay strong while we remain victims.*[41] Dizzee Rascal also raps about the failures of government. In the song 'Dirtee Cash' (2009), he asks the government if it has any solution to end the possession of guns, use of drugs and prostitution: *Everywhere I go, there's a girl on the corner / Guns*

39 Dr. Dre, 'Still D.R.E.' (2000), referring to drive-by shootings, AK-47 automatic rifles, forced sexual intercourse in prison, weed and traffic in low quality drugs, respectively.

40 'White America' (2002).

41 'Mr Prime Minister' (2005).

and drugs got the city like a sauna / And its getting warmer and out of order / Turn a poor struggling mother to a mourner / Mister politician, can you tell me the solution / What's the answer, what's the conclusion.

Criticism of the government often goes together with criticizing the tax system. This is a popular theme among English rappers. In the song 'Work Work' (2008), N-Dubz raps that many families are left with very little money and are unable to afford food: *See me I scream for the scrape my taxman rape / Government wonderin' why we show hate / When there's kids sayin' mummy I'm starving, hungry, need food in my tummy / Mammas crying out loud now, cos' she don't got no money.* However, unlike their American counterparts, English hip-hop artists seem to keep faith in the power of institutions to remedy these problems. Plan B for example criticizes the government for the lack of facilities available to the youth: *It's ironic don't you think, that 5 years back the same cats are now on crack / They didn't even used to drink, now they're the missing links / In the world of wasted talent could have been great, now they're just making up the balance / Musicians, artists, writers, authors, gymnasts athletes footballers / Bare peeps I used to know that could've turned pro, now the only game they play is the one on road / Whether it be drug pushin', shoplifting or prostitution, some sort of institution seems like the only solution.*[42]

4.3.4 *Respect: No Dissing*

Perhaps the most important principle of hip-hop law is to respect others within the community. While there is virtually no need to take into account the interests of society as a whole or of (people in) other segments of society, there is a high standard of respect to be paid vis-à-vis others in the 'hip-hop community'. The threshold for being disrespected, or *dissed*, is relatively low; rappers feel insulted more quickly than an average person. Any infringement on somebody's reputation or pride cannot be tolerated. Dr. Dre's song 'Fuck Wit Dre Day' (1992) is one long message to the outside world that he should not be disrespected: *Now understand this, my nigga Dre can't be touched (…) Cause when you diss Dre you diss yourself, motherfucker.* This concern with disrespect is to be found in a wide variety of lyrics, including those of Ludacris (*Want to disrespect give me your neck / And I'll put a knife on it*[43]) and Jay-Z (*No disrespect to you, make sure your word is true*[44]).

There are various ways to earn respect. One is to make money, but it is even more important to do so by breaking the law. The lyrics suggest that the more one engages in criminal conduct and contributes to one's street credibility ('street cred'), the more respect one deserves. This is not surprising in view of what was seen in Section 4.3.2

42 'Missing Links' (2006).
43 'Cold Outside' (2001).
44 'Politics As Usual' (1996).

– breaking the law is a legitimate form of revolting against the status quo.[45] This also explains why hip-hop lyrics are sympathetic to prisoners.[46] It is not difficult to see the importance of gaining and enforcing respect within the community; if one does not feel treated as a human being by the regular State institutions, one needs to find alternative ways of recognition. The obligation not to disrespect others in the hip-hop community is one of these: it partly replaces the 'normal' human dignity one is entitled to vis-à-vis the State and anyone else.[47]

Although respect has a very broad scope, it is possible to refine it based on sociological research carried out within street gangs active in American cities.[48] The lyrics confirm the results of this research that one of the main principles is honesty and the need to keep one's word. One example from a Jay-Z lyric was given above, but many other examples exist. Another main principle is not to badmouth someone, or say bad things about someone behind his back, reflecting a high level of loyalty to others within the community. If Dr. Dre feels his reputation and pride are affected by somebody else, his reaction is clear: *Oh, don't think I forgot, let you slide. Let me ride, just another homicide.*[49] In a mainstream perception of law, murder as retaliation for an oral insult may be disproportionate, but not so in hip-hop law in which 'dissing' is one of the most severe crimes imaginable.

Another illustration of the importance of not dissing others can be found in the absolute prohibition of snitching. To provide information to the police is seen as unacceptable, even if this means that one will be jailed for the rest of one's life. Or, as Jay-Z states: *I will never tell, even if it means sittin' in a cell.*[50] In Jay-Z's 'A Week Ago' (1998), the main character's partner starts 'dropping names' to the police: *I'm mad at myself cause I didn't spot the weakling / I would've bet the house you wouldn't speak a thing.* The consequence of this equates to being banned from the community: *The labelling of a snitch is a lifetime scar / You'll always be in jail nigga, just minus the bars.* This lesson was well understood by the rapper Lil' Kim (Kimberly Denise Jones, born New York City 1974), who served a one-year prison sentence for perjury after having lied to a federal jury about the involvement of a friend in a shooting in Manhattan in 2001.[51]

45 Cf. Butler, *Stanford Law Review* 56 (2004), at 997-998, who defines this as a 'glorification of outlaws.'

46 See also Butler, *Stanford Law Review* 56 (2004), at 1002, who quotes Angie Stone ('Brotha', 2001): *To everyone of y'all behind bars / You know that Angie loves ya.*

47 On the philosophical origins of human dignity: P. Lee & R.P. George, 'The Nature and Basis of Human Dignity', *Ratio Juris* 21 (2008) 173.

48 Cf. M. Knox, *Gangsta in the House*, Houston 1995.

49 'Fuck With Dre Day' (1996).

50 'Justify My Thug' (2003).

51 See J. Vineyard, 'Lil' Kim found guilty of lying to Grand Jury', MTV News 17 May 2005, available at www.mtv.com/news/articles/1498251/lil-kim-convicted-perjury-conspiracy.jhtml.

4.3.5 Instrumental Use of the Law

The final principle of hip-hop law discussed in this chapter is about the way in which the law itself is used. Hip-hop does not see the law primarily as protecting essential community values and norms (guaranteeing the rule of law), but much more as a means to an end.[52] The lyrics even suggest very clearly that this 'end' is some personal benefit – the law should be used to profit from when it is to one's advantage, but can be easily ignored in any other case.

We have already seen many examples of disobeying the law. Examples of lyrics in which the law is used to the advantage of the portrayed person are provided by Eminem. In the partly autobiographical song 'Without Me' (2002), he victoriously shouts: *I just settled all my lawsuits, Fuck you Debbie.* Eminem here refers to the lawsuit filed by his mother, Debbie Mathers, who sued him for a total amount of 11 million dollars in reputation damages.[53] Another case in which Eminem shows his faith in the legal system, and feels good about the law when it is on his side, is in 'Hailie's Song' (2002). He just won the case regarding the custody of his daughter and states: *My baby's travelled back to the arms of her rightful owner.* Rappers also enthusiastically invoke their rights when being halted by the police, revealing a sophisticated level of knowledge about the law's practical implications. In Jay-Z's '99 Problems', the main character is driving around with 'raw' (slang for uncut heroin or cocaine) in the trunk of his car when being halted for speeding by the police: *License and registration and step out of the car / Are you carrying a weapon on you, I know a lot of you are / I ain't stepping out of shit, all my paper's legit / Well, do you mind if I look round the car a little bit? / Well my glove compartment is locked, so is the trunk in the back / And I know my rights, so you gon' need a warrant for that.* When the officer asks him whether he is some kind of lawyer, Jay-Z replies: *Nah, I ain't pass the bar, but I know a little bit / Enough that you won't illegally search my shit.*[54]

It is interesting to see that the mainstream view of the law becomes more prominent when rappers grow older and richer. They were critical of the law when they still lived 'in the hood', but this changes with growing wealth and the potential to make use of the law in the way that suits them best. In Jay-Z's 'A Week Ago' (1998), the main character raps: *Seventeen and I'm holding on to around a mill / I could bail out and blow trial and come around on appeal.* Although the song's hero is only 17, he already has a million dollars and can hire a good lawyer and post bail. After that he can just 'blow trial', meaning that he will not appear for his scheduled trial date,

52 See on this distinction e.g. B.Z. Tamanaha, *Law as a Means to an End*, Cambridge 2006. See also Butler, *Stanford Law Review* 56 (2004), at 990.

53 Case 1999-003915-NZ *Mathers, Briggs D v. Mathers, III, Marshall B DMD* and case 2000-003366-NZ *Mathers, Briggs D v. Mathers, III, Marshall B DMD.* Information retrieved via http://macombcountymi.gov/pa.

54 See also e.g. 50 Cent's 'High All The Time' (2003).

and win the case on appeal. Eminem also realizes the value of the law for the rich: in 'Saying Goodbye To Hollywood' (2002), he raps: *I just sold two million records, I don't need to go to jail / I'm not about to lose my freedom over no female.* Dr. Dre is even more explicit; years after his first album 'The Chronic' (1992), he suggests that violence is no longer for him, so he will not challenge a new generation of outlaws and be a family man instead.[55]

4.4 Conclusions: A Law to Survive in the Urban Jungle?

This chapter offers an inventory and analysis of how the law is perceived in a representative sample of hip-hop lyrics. Our analysis shows that four main principles would be part of a legal system designed by hip-hop artists. First, criminal justice is based on the age-old adage of an eye for an eye, reflecting the desire to retaliate proportionately against any offense. Second, self-justice and self-government reign supreme in a hip-hop version of the law – instead of waiting for an inaccurate community response, it is allowed to take the law into one's own hands. Third, there is an overriding obligation to respect anyone else within the hip-hop community, meaning that any 'dissing' is not allowed and will be severely punished. Finally, the law is seen as an instrument to be used to one's advantage wherever possible and to be ignored if not considered useful.

The question remains what overall view of justice the lyrics reflect. We believe that Professor Green is a keen observer of the philosophy underlying the four principles. In his song 'Jungle' (2010), he raps that there is no point in being a law-abiding citizen in a city in which it is all about the survival of the fittest by preying on the weak. He sings that particularly on council estates people act like animals and stab, shoot and beat each other. *I see no point in living life that right, so I just take what I can find (...) Welcome to Hackney, a place where I think somebody's been playing Jumanji*[56] */ A Manor where man are like animals, an' they'll yam on you like they yam on food / Cats with claws that'll stab a yout', act bad an' catch a slap or two.* His American colleague 50 Cent also refers to a jungle-like society: *So chances are, I'ma have to blast me a nigga / I'm on that kevlar vest shit, that wild wild west shit.*[57] If we look at the law as a way to survive, setting and enforcing norms that allow people to make a living and to be protected against crime, the absence of this type of protection prompts the need to survive in another way. The four principles reflect this; they come to the

55 See already the song 'Bang Bang' (2000) as well as S. Michaels, Dr Dre says Detox will be his final album, *The Guardian* 23 November 2010, available through www.guardian.co.uk.

56 Jumanji refers to the 1981 children's book, 1995 film and 1996-1999 television series about a magical board game that implements animals and other jungle elements as the players are playing the game.

57 'I'm supposed to die tonight' (2005).

surface in the absence of laws that are State-enforced and regarded as fair by the community. In this respect, hip-hop law shows an interesting parallel with societies in which there is no effective government control to be relied upon by the citizens. The norms prevailing in the American Wild West offer an example. This 'Code of the West' entailed that one could violate any State law as long as one upheld the unwritten Code among cowmen. Violation led to the grave sanction of becoming an outcast and, as a consequence, to having a lesser chance of surviving.[58]

Seen from this perspective, each of the identified principles contributes to survival in a lawless community (or one that is experienced as such by its inhabitants). This needs little explanation for the principles of an eye for an eye and of self-justice, but also the high degree of respect due to fellow community members adds to one's survival; it helps to create a closer community of people one can unconditionally trust. In a society without enforced State law, there is a need to replace the law with clear indications of a person's good will; not dissing anyone can be seen as such. The fourth principle is not consistent with a mainstream view of the law, but it can also be readily explained as arising out of the need to survive in the urban jungle – the use of the law to one's advantage is not based on some moral consideration, but simply on the fact that one profits from it.

58 See R.F. Adams, *The Cowman & His Code of Ethics*, Austin 1969. Also substantively, the Code in part resembles our principles by emphasizing the importance of honesty (your word is your bond) and loyalty.

5 The Phylogeny of the Unpaid Seller's Right to Vindicate Goods: A Test Study*

5.1 Introduction

A well-known controversy concerns the origins and subsequent development of the so-called 'price payment rule'. This rule makes the transfer of movable property dependent on the buyer's payment of the price. While modern transfer systems are usually categorized on the basis of whether transfer takes place upon the conclusion of the contract (consensual systems) or upon the delivery of the good (tradition systems),[1] clear signs in legal sources ranging over a period of more than 2000 years indicate that in a third type of transfer system, payment of the price is a necessary requirement for the property to pass. The Institutes of Justinian (533 AD) provide the best-known example of this system.[2] Modern traces of the price payment rule can be found in jurisdictions such as France, the Netherlands, Québec and Louisiana that all give the seller the right to vindicate unpaid goods for a short period of time after delivery.

There is a long-standing debate among legal historians on which jurisdictions exactly accepted the price payment rule and on how the rule developed over time. This debate deals in particular with the extent to which post-12th century applications of the rule can be traced back to the influence of Roman law or have their origins in local indigenous laws. The arguments used in this debate are based on the traditional methods of philological and legal analysis (including interpolation critique) and are aimed at the classification of similar variations of the rule appearing in different geographical parts of Europe (and sometimes beyond). However, it cannot be said that this led to an undisputed reconstruction of the origins and genesis ('reception') of a third system of property transfer since the Middle Ages. Its exact development remains something of a mystery.[3] This may also be caused by the great

* The tables, figures and dataset are available at https://dataverse.nl/dataset.xhtml?persistentId=hdl:10411/PISBWE.

1 See e.g. M. Hinteregger & L. van Vliet, Transfer, in *Cases, Materials and Text on Property Law: Ius Commune Casebooks*, Oxford 2012, 783 ff.

2 Inst. 2.1.41; see further below, Section 5.2.

3 H. Honsell, Th. Mayer-Maly & W. Selb, in P. Jörs, W. Kunkel & L. Wenger, *Römisches Recht*, 4. Aufl., Berlin 1987, 161: 'lebhaft umstritten' and 'ein nicht ganz schlüssiges Entwicklungsbild.'

many instances of the rule to be found around the world, all showing small variations in detail.

This chapter aims to shed new light on the contested history of the price payment rule. It does so by testing a novel method of analysis that was until now not used in analysing legal materials. This method is based on computational phylogenetics, the quantitative study of the evolutionary history of organisms. Computational phylogenetic analysis was originally developed in the field of biology where it is used to evaluate heritable traits, such as DNA sequences, with a view to building trees showing the evolutionary relationships among different species.[4] In recent years, this method was also increasingly used to study non-biological entities, including texts, folk songs, languages and traditions, as well as archaeological objects such as textiles and buildings.[5] One widely publicized[6] contribution by anthropologist Jamie Tehrani shows how powerful this method is when it comes to analysing cross-cultural relationships among folktales. Tehrani investigated 58 different versions of the story of *Little Red Riding Hood* in order to establish whether these stories evolved from one common ancestor or not.[7]

Tehrani's work shows the potential for computational phylogenetics in legal analysis. Law is not any different from genes, languages, fairy tales and other cultural phenomena in the way it evolves. Much like these other phenomena, legal rules develop by dropping some features and taking on new ones as they spread to different parts of the world over time. Put differently, the law is also subject to mutation, replication, inheritance and selection. This insight as such is not new; even before Darwin, law was looked at as a system subject to evolutionary change.[8] What is new, though, is the insight that evolution can be studied with the computational tools biologists use to track genetic evolution. This can provide, in another way than through traditional historical analysis, the evidence that some rules are 'sisters or cousins' while others are more like 'mother and son', or simply lack a common ancestor. The price payment rule seems an excellent test case to show this potential now that the many variations of this rule are likely to have emerged as a result of descent with modification.[9] The

4 See on phylogeny in general E.O. Wiley & B.S. Lieberman, *Phylogenetics: Theory and Practice of Phylogenetic Systematics*, 2nd ed., Hoboken 2011 and on quantitative methods T. Warnow, *Computational Phylogenetics*, Cambridge 2017.

5 References to be found in C.J. Howe & H.F. Windram, 'Phylomemetics – Evolutionary Analysis beyond the Gene', *PLoS Biol* 9 (2011), e1001069.

6 See e.g. The Evolution of *Little Red Riding Hood*, *Science* 14 November 2013, www.sciencemag.org/news/2013/11/evolution-little-red-riding-hood, What Wide Origins You Have, Little Red Riding Hood!, *National Geographic* 30 November 2013, http://news.nationalgeographic.com/news/2013/11/131129-little-red-riding-hood-folktale-tehrani-anthropology-science and (in Dutch) Variaties op een grote boze wolf, *NRC Handelsblad* 21 December 2013, www.nrc.nl/nieuws/2013/12/21/variaties-op-een-grote-boze-wolf-1328116-a214776.

7 J.J. Tehrani, 'The Phylogeny of Little Red Riding Hood', *PLoS One* 8 (2013), e78871.

8 Cf. E.D. Elliott, 'The Evolutionary Tradition in Jurisprudence', *Columbia Law Review* 85 (1985) 38.

9 As in the case of folk tales: Tehrani, *PLoS One* 8 (2013), at 2.

aim of this chapter is thus to test whether phylogenetic analysis can take us any further in understanding the genesis of the price payment rule. If so, the method has the potential to also be useful in analysing other legal rules. In this sense, the ambition of this chapter goes beyond the narrow confines of the history of sales law and aims to explore a new method in legal scholarship in general.

The argument unfolds as follows. Section 5.2 provides a concise comparative and historical overview of jurisdictions in which traces of the price payment rule can be found. This overview is partly based on previous work by legal historians, but it adds a new comparative overview of modern jurisdictions in which the price payment rule can be found. This section also sketches some of the current controversies over the development of the rule. Section 5.3 outlines the proposed novel method to analyse the legal materials and refutes potential objections to this method. It also further limits the scope of the research and explains the dataset. Section 5.4 shows the provisional results, while the final Section 5.5 draws some conclusions. This does not mean that the current analysis is brought to completion; the aim of this chapter – to be seen as a test study – is more to show the potential of the new method than to make use of all possibilities that computational phylogenetics has to offer.

5.2 The Price Payment Rule: A Comparative-Historical Overview

The historical origins of the price payment rule are usually attributed to the Institutes of Justinian (533 AD).[10] Inst. 2.1.41[11] clearly states that goods delivered under a contract of sale only become the property of the buyer if the latter paid the price or gave 'satisfaction' in another way, such as through providing personal or real security. Only in case the seller gave credit to the buyer (*'fidem emptoris secutus fuerit'*), usually understood to mean that the seller delivered the good in confidence that the buyer would pay the price, ownership passed immediately. While the contents of this rule are relatively clear, its origins are not. The Institutes themselves attribute the rule to the law of the Twelve Tables (450 BC), but the modern view is that this cannot have been the case.[12] It is also unlikely that the Justinian rule finds its direct

10 The main source of information on the historical development of the price payment rule is still R. Feenstra, *Reclame en revindicatie*, PhD Amsterdam 1949, Haarlem 1949, summarized and updated in e.g. R. Feenstra, 'Eigendomsovergang bij koop en terugvorderingsrecht van de onbetaalde verkoper: Romeins recht en Middeleeuws handelsrecht', *Tydskrif vir Hedendaagse Romeins-Hollandse Reg* 50 (1987) 127. Recent overviews also in R. Zimmermann, *The Law of Obligations*, Cape Town 1990, 274 ff. and T. Rüfner, '*Traditio* und Kaufpreiszahlung in *Ius Commune* und *Common Law*', in E. Jakab & W. Ernst (Hrsg.), *Kaufen nach Römischem recht*, Berlin 2008, 233, at 246 ff.

11 See Annex 1, no. 30.

12 See e.g. Honsell, Mayer-Maly & Selb 1987, 161-163.

basis in classical Roman law (0-250 BC),[13] even though several sources in the Digest hint at the acceptance of the price payment rule already in this period.[14] There are indications, on the other hand, that a similar rule existed in ancient Greece as evidenced by a fragment attributed to Theophrastus (4th century BC).[15] In one view, there is a direct link between this text and the acceptance of the price payment rule in Byzantine times.[16]

The exact development of the price payment rule during the reception of Roman law is also uncertain. The debate among legal historians focuses on the question of whether the local variations of the rule allowing an unpaid seller to vindicate the goods, as they emerged from the 12th century onward, are derived from Roman law, are based on indigenous local laws or are a combination of both. Annex 1 lists almost 30 variations (*taxa*) of the price payment rule in Latin, Dutch, French and Italian in the period between 1161 and 1794. The specific difficulty with many of these sources is that they are interpolated; although the price payment rule most probably had a basis in local customary laws, the learned jurists made it seem as if they were derived from Roman law in order to enhance their legitimacy. This makes it difficult to trace their exact provenance.

Feenstra points out that it was not easy to give a Romanist flavour to the indigenous rules.[17] One difficulty the learned jurists faced was that the local laws often only protected the unpaid seller in case of the buyer's insolvency, while Roman law makes no mention of this requirement at all. Another problem was that the rules from the 12th century onwards also allowed the seller to vindicate unpaid goods in case he had given credit to the buyer (*fidem sequi*), a clear violation of the Justinian rule we have seen before. The ingenuous construction to avoid too much of a contradiction with the original Roman sources was not to regard a sale as one on credit if the buyer was given only a short period of time (of, for example, ten days) to pay the purchase price.[18] Another invention to make the local laws better fit the Roman example was to hold that, even in the case that credit had been given, the seller could reclaim the

13 Honsell, Mayer-Maly & Selb 1987, 163. For an elaborate overview of opinions on this matter: J.A.C. Thomas, 'Institutes 2.1.41 and the Passage of Property on Sale', *South African Law Journal* 90 (1973) 150.

14 See in particular D 18.1.19 (Pomponius), listed in Annex 1 as no. 29 and D 18.1.53 (Gaius). Details in Zimmermann, *The Law of Obligations*, 274 ff.

15 Stobaeus, Florilegium 44.22; on its potential influence on Roman law: F. Pringsheim, *Der Kauf mit fremdem Geld*, Leipzig 1916, 70 ff., disputed by Feenstra 1949, 60 ff. Cf. Zimmermann, *The Law of Obligations*, 275.

16 F. Pringsheim, *Der Kauf mit fremdem Geld*, Leipzig 1916, 70 ff.

17 R. Feenstra, 'De Romeinsrechtelijke prijsbetalingsregel en het recht van reclame van artikel 7:39-44 BW', *Ars Aequi* 55 (2006) 876, at 881 ff., largely based on Feenstra, *Reclame en revindicatie*, 98 ff.

18 See e.g. Statutes of Amsterdam of 1658 (Annex 1, no. 42). See for this development from a different angle – that of protection of the innocent subsequent purchaser – D.L. Carey Miller, 'Transfer of Ownership', in R. Feenstra & R. Zimmermann (eds.), *Das römisch-holländische Recht*, Berlin 1992, 521, at 533.

goods for the reason that non-payment (often coinciding with the seller fleeing and insolvency) undid the given credit.[19]

Despite these difficulties, legal historians categorized the variations of the price payment rule into separate groups on the basis of their common characteristics. Among these are whether insolvency of the buyer is required (as in the local statutes of Pisa 1161, Siena 1262 and Albenga 1281), whether the protection of the seller is based on a special lien[20] sometimes referred to as a right of pledge (as in Marseille 1253 and Sassari 1316) or simply on (retained) ownership (as in Albenga 1281, Zeeland 1495 and Groningen 1701) and on whether a time limit exists for exercising the right by the seller (as in Roman-Dutch law, with still many variations as to the exact length of this time period). Section 5.3 will show that it is still possible to categorize the variations on the basis of many other criteria.

Traces of the price payment rule can also be found in the current law. Annex 1 lists more than 15 jurisdictions that still accept the rule in one form or another. The most obvious applications are the laws of France, Belgium, Luxembourg, the Netherlands, Italy, Romania, South Africa, Québec and Louisiana. They all allow the unpaid seller to claim back the goods within a time period ranging between 8 and 60 days. All these rules are clearly influenced by each other, with a special role for the French Civil Code that – except in South Africa – was taken as the model jurisdiction. Lithuania and Bulgaria offer comparable rules. Some other jurisdictions, including Norway, Hungary, the United Kingdom, China and Japan, adopted statutes aiming to protect the seller of unpaid goods still in transit ('stoppage in transitu'). These rules allow the seller to stop the transport of goods already handed over to the carrier, but not yet to the transferee.[21] This should not conceal that, when looked at from a European perspective, only a minority of modern jurisdictions accept the price payment rule in one form or another. The Romano-Germanic legal family does not adopt it at all,[22] while only some French-based jurisdictions still do.[23] This may explain why the rule was not inserted in the DCFR.[24] At the same time, of the jurisdictions that do accept it, quite a few enacted it in both their civil and commercial code, again with varying requirements as to when exactly the right can be invoked.

19 See e.g. Statutes of Antwerp of 1608 (Annex 1, no. 48).

20 An 'obligation spéciale', on which Feenstra, *Ars Aequi* 55 (2006), at 881.

21 Cf. C. Von Bar & E. Clive (eds.), *Principles, Definitions and Model Rules of European Private Law: Draft Common Frame of Reference (DCFR)*, Vol. 5, Munich 2009, Comment F to Art. VIII.-2:201 DCFR. The DCFR lacks a rule on the right of stoppage in transit.

22 Interestingly, the 1868 (Art. 1585) and 1967 (Art. 886) Civil Code of Portugal – both influenced by German doctrine – explicitly deny the action to the seller.

23 Scots law also does not accept the rule. See D. Johnston, 'Sale and Transfer of Title in Roman and Scots Law', in A.D.E. Lewis & D.J. Ibbetson (eds.), *The Roman Law Tradition*, Cambridge 1994, 182 ff.

24 The rule is mentioned in *DCFR* 2009, Note 13 to Art. IV.A.-4:101 and in Comment C (d) to Art. VIII.-2:101.

5.3 Phylogenetic Analysis: Dataset and Methodology

5.3.1 Introduction

This section explains the proposed phylogenetic method used to analyse the existing variations of the price payment rule. The essence of this method is to look at the variations as being based on mutation by descent, thus allowing to reconstruct a family tree showing their mutual relationships. This fresh perspective can offer various advantages compared to the traditional historical-legal method based on qualitative textual analysis. First, the reconstruction is not based on chronology, region or frequency. The fact that a known variation is older (e.g., can be found in the Roman Digest), originates from some part of Europe (e.g., Italy) or occurs more frequently (e.g., the right can be enforced both in and outside of the buyer's insolvency) does not imply that this is the ancestral form. The traditional method only allows studying the variations that were found, not those that disappeared. The phylogenetic method can thus undo a bias for Roman origins of variations of the price payment rule occurring after the beginning of the 12th century. Second, the method allows one to consider all differences and similarities among the variations, whereas current scholarship tends to focus on only a few (such as the period within which vindication must take place and whether insolvency is a requirement or not[25]).[26]

This does not mean that applying phylogenetic analysis to law is unproblematic. Apart from general objections against the use of quantitative data in law – to be dismissed now that quantitative analysis is simply an *alternative* method of analysis, not one that seeks to replace textual exploration or normative considerations[27] – a potential difficulty is that in law the transmission of traits often takes place horizontally. Unlike genes, legal rules tend to travel from one country to another within the same time period. It could be argued therefore that a network model[28] would better fit the facts than a tree model.[29] This argument, however, does not fit the specific example of the price payment rule as it in fact developed over a long period of time. Also, the fact that legal rules, like languages, change more rapidly than genes, or that selection is steered by changing societal views and not by the environment in the strict sense of the word, pose no fundamental problems for phylogenetic analysis in law.[30]

---

25 See e.g. E. Rabel, *Das Recht des Warenkaufs*, Bd. 2, Berlin 1958, 40 ff.

26 Tehrani, *PLoS One* 8 (2013), at 2.

27 Cf. M. Siems, *Comparative Law*, Cambridge 2014, 146 ff.

28 Cf. G. van Dijck, *MoneyLaw (and Beyond)*, The Hague 2017, 15 ff.

29 See for this argument in the case of language transmission H. Luqman, *A Phylogenetic Approach to Comparative Linguistics: A Test Study using the Languages of Borneo*, research paper NHM, Imperial College London 2010, 2.

30 Cf. Luqman, research paper NHM 2010, 2.

5.3.2 The Dataset

The dataset consists of 56 variations of the price payment rule drafted between the years 150 and 2006. They originate from 41 different jurisdictions written in 13 languages (Annex 1). The separate list of texts (Annex 1) provides the full list, with English translations of texts not in Latin script. The online version provides translations into English of all texts not in Dutch, English, French, German, Italian or Latin. The dataset is based on extensive research in secondary sources as well as on a systematic search in a large number of civil codes.[31] Figure 5.1 shows a map of the provenance of these texts in Europe.

Figure 5.1 Map of provenance of texts in Europe

The choice was made to limit the dataset to texts that served, or still serve, as legislative provisions (the great majority of the texts in Annex 1) or consist of authoritative judicial decisions in case-based or mixed jurisdictions. Statements on the

31 Facilitated by English translations of codes available at http://landwise.resourceequity.org.

price payment rule by learned authors are therefore excluded, even though they may describe the laws of their time. This explains why the Theophrastus fragment on Greek sales law mentioned above is excluded, as is the rule on price payment in the 9th-century *Lex Romana Raetica Curiensis.*[32] It also explains why Hugo Grotius' *Introduction to the Jurisprudence of Holland* of 1631 is not included in the dataset,[33] even though it contains a flawless expression of the price payment rule similar to Inst. 2.1.41.[34] Provisions literally copied from a 'mother jurisdiction', as in the case of former colonies, were also excluded.[35] Local statutes similar to others are not part of the dataset, which explains why, for example, the statutes of Leiden 1659 and Haarlem 1710 were not included – they are similar to those of Amsterdam 1658 (no. 42).

Also excluded were legislative provisions merely making the payment of the price dependent on the transfer of property[36] or abstaining from making a direct link between vindication and non-payment. An example of the latter is the Manava Dharmasastra of 200 BCE, stating: "After buying or selling anything, if someone here regrets his decision, he takes back that article within ten days."[37] Provisions about retention of ownership ('reservation of title') were also excluded as these do not provide the seller with a default statutory right. This means that the Austrian § 1063 ABGB is not part of the dataset, even though an 'implied reservation of title' is accepted by various authors who assume that in case parties agree to perform simultaneously but only the seller performs, ownership does not pass. The Austrian *Oberster Gerichtshof* never accepted this *kurzfristiger Eigentumsvorbehalt.*[38]

---

32 RC 18.9: 'si ... carta receperit et precium non dederit, ipsa carta reddat et insuper ipsum precium ... det.' See *Monumenta Germaniae Historica, Leges* V (ed. K. Zeumer), Hannover 1875-1889. Cf. E. Levy, *West Roman Vulgar Law: The Law of Property*, Philadelphia 1951, 131 ff. On other early systems: U. Von Lübtow, 'Studien zum altrömischen Kaufrecht', in *Festschrift Koschaker*, Bd. II, Weimar 1939, 113, at 134.

33 Although this choice can be disputed; in 1859 the South African Republic of Transvaal declared Grotius' *Introduction* to be the applicable law, albeit only as secondary authority after Joannes Van der Linden's *Regsgeleerd practicaal en koopmanshandboek*. See also Vinnius, *Institutiones*, Lib. II, Tit. I, 41 and Voet, *Commentarius ad Pandectas*, Lib. VI, Tit. I, 14 ff.

34 II.5.14: 'Doch wat levering aengaat die op koop volgt van tilbaer goed, staet te letten dat daer mede den eigendom niet over en gaet, 't en zij den kooper de kooppenning heeft betaelt, ofte den verkooper daer voor zeecker gedaen, of dat hem de verkooper de selve penningen heeft geborgt.'

35 As in the case of the civil codes of Indonesia 1847 and Surinam 1869. The French provisions were literally taken over in the codes of e.g. Haiti 1825 and Bolivia 1831 (as in Togo, Cameroon, Madagascar and Niger), while the UK Sale of Goods Act was adopted in many other jurisdictions within the British Commonwealth.

36 See e.g. Art. 507 s. 1 of the Civil Code of Armenia of 1998: "Unless otherwise provided by the contract, the purchaser becomes the owner of goods from the time of payment for the goods."

37 P. Olivelle (ed.), *Manu's Code of Law*, Oxford 2004, 179.

38 W. Faber & B. Lurger (eds.), *National Reports on the Transfer of Movables in Europe*, Vol. 1, München 2008, 103 ff.; E.-M. Kieninger (ed.), *Security Rights in Movable Property in European Private Law*, Cambridge 2004, 176 seems to accept this doctrinal view as the positive law.

For the sake of this chapter, the scope of the price payment rule is limited to those cases in which the buyer's non-payment of the price allows the seller to vindicate[39] goods that were already delivered under the contract, or are still in transit. With this, two types of rights are excluded from the analysis: the right of the seller to retain the goods until the price is paid and the seller's privileged priority position in collective insolvency proceeding. The first right, also known as the unpaid seller's lien or right of retention, is an application of the broader right to withhold performance and can only be exercised in case the goods are still held by the seller. The second right (so-called *privilège*, *preferencia* or *Vorrecht*) has close historic links to the price payment rule,[40] but is not a right of vindication – an owner cannot have a privilege on his own property. The privilege only assigns the seller a specific priority among the rights of other creditors in case of the buyer's insolvency. Only in so far as the price payment rule allows the seller to vindicate goods from an insolvent buyer – outside of collective proceedings[41] – is the right included in the dataset.

5.3.3 *Coding of the Characteristics*

The used texts in the dataset (Annex 1) are analysed on the basis of 16 different characteristics (Annex 2). The coding of these traits took place on the basis of the original text of the provision. Only a clear and undisputed judicial or doctrinal interpretation or a later statutory change prevailed over the original text. For example, Art. 1191 Dutch Civil Code 1838 (no. 2) was supplemented in 1935 with a new provision Art. 1192a in order to protect bona fide purchasers. This means that in coding NLBW1838, trait 6 was coded as '1' ('not if bona fide buyer/buyer sine fraude'). In the case of the Roman sources, a particular difficulty in coding was the extent to which interpolations have influenced the Roman sources or not (in particular relevant in coding no. 29 and no. 30). Here the text was followed as closely as possible. In interpreting the medieval Dutch, French and Italian statutes, the interpretations of Feenstra were followed.[42] Another difficulty concerned the coding of characteristic 1, dealing with the doctrinal basis for recovery of the good. While some texts make an explicit reference to retained ownership or tacit security (pledge, *vindication pignoris* or the *obligation spéciale* set out by Feenstra[43]), most texts are unclear or even silent

39 Meaning: with 'real' (proprietary) effect. Jurisdictions use different terms to describe the right, such as *révendication* in French law and *recht van reclame* in Dutch law (on which H.A.G. Fikkers, *Recht van reclame*, Deventer 1992). V. Sagaert, 'Consensual versus Delivery Systems', in W. Faber & B. Lurger (eds.), *Rules for the Transfer of Movables: A Candidate for European Harmonisation of National Reforms?*, München 2008, 43 uses the term 'quasi-revendication.'

40 On which Rabel, *Das Recht des Warenkaufs*, 40 ff. and L.D. Cromwell, 'Vendor's Privilege: Adheret Visceribus Rei', *Louisiana Law Review* 75 (2015) 1169.

41 As is possible in French law (Art. L 624-9 ff. C.Com).

42 Feenstra, *Reclame en revindicatie*, 159 ff.

43 Feenstra, id., 101 and Feenstra, *Ars Aequi* 55 (2006), at 881.

about this. Despite speculations about the origins of the provisions in the Dutch civil codes of 1809 and 1838 being based on tacit security,[44] textual interpretation led to a coding as 'no explicit mention'. Only the French civil code of 1804 (no. 5) and the Romanian one of 1864 (no. 12) were coded as being based on tacit security. The full data matrix is provided in Table 2 (available online).

5.3.4 *Phylogenetic Methods Used*

The aim of the analysis employed in this chapter is to establish to what extent the 56 variations of the price payment rule are phylogenetically distinct. This requires a method of phylogenetic inference for the evaluation of the 16 different traits, leading to a diagram that hypothesizes about the evolutionary ancestry of the species (in our case the texts) or *taxa*. Often used computational methods of inference to build such a phylogenetic tree are parsimony, maximum likelihood (ML) and Bayesian inference.[45] This chapter does not carry out a full systematic analysis,[46] but aims to show the potential of phylogenetic analysis in tracing the history of the price payment rule.

The main programme used in the present analysis is Mesquite, a software programme designed to help biologists organize data about organisms.[47] Mesquite's character matrix editor was used to insert the data in a file in NEXUS format. This file was used to create several trees. First, a Mesquite heuristic search was done to create the most parsimonious tree with settings on Treelength, Stored Matrices, SPR Rearranger and MAXTREES 100. This led to an unrooted tree shown in Figure 5.2 as a square line tree. Such an unrooted tree plots the relationships between the variations without assuming anything about their descent. Figure 5.3 shows the same results, but now as a rooted tree with Inst533 defined as the outgroup (used as the point of comparison for all other data). A rooted tree identifies a most recent common ancestor and shows the distances of the variations from the root (represented by the branch lengths). Subsequently, a majority rule consensus tree was created, unrooted in Figure 5.4 and again rooted in Inst533 in Figure 5.5. A majority rule consensus tree is based on only the traits that are present in the majority of the trees. It presents a single representative tree showing the most likely relationship among the variations. The graphs are reproduced in Section 5.4, followed by an analysis of what they entail.

44 Feenstra, *Reclame en revindicatie*, 101.
45 Cf. D.A. Baum & S.D. Smith, *Three Thinking: An Introduction to Phylogenetic Biology*, Greenwood Village 2012.
46 For an example of how to do this: Tehrani, *PLoS One* 8 (2013) 2, using cladistics, Bayesian interference and NeighbourNet.
47 W.P. Maddison & D.R. Maddison, *Mesquite: A Modular System for Evolutionary Analysis*, 2009, version 3.31, http://mesquiteproject.org.

5.4 Results of the Analysis

The four trees described in Section 5.3.4 above look as follows.[48]

Figure 5.2 Unrooted tree (heuristic search)

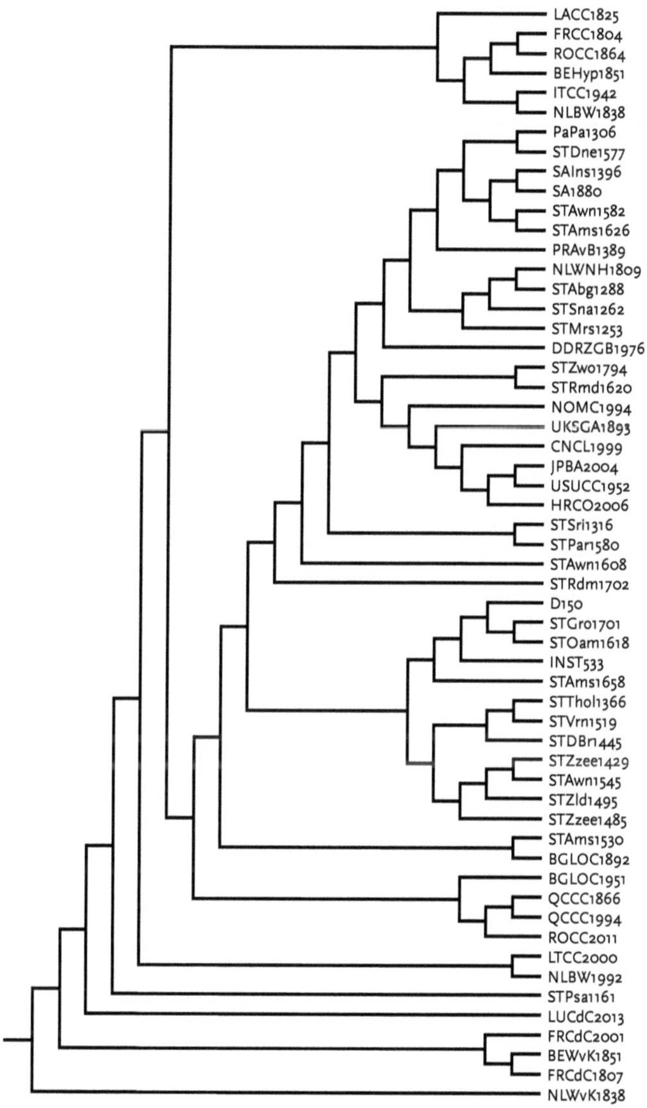

48 Versions in higher resolution are available at https://dataverse.nl/dataset.xhtml?persistentId=hdl:10411/PISBWE.

Figure 5.3 Rooted tree with Inst533 as outgroup

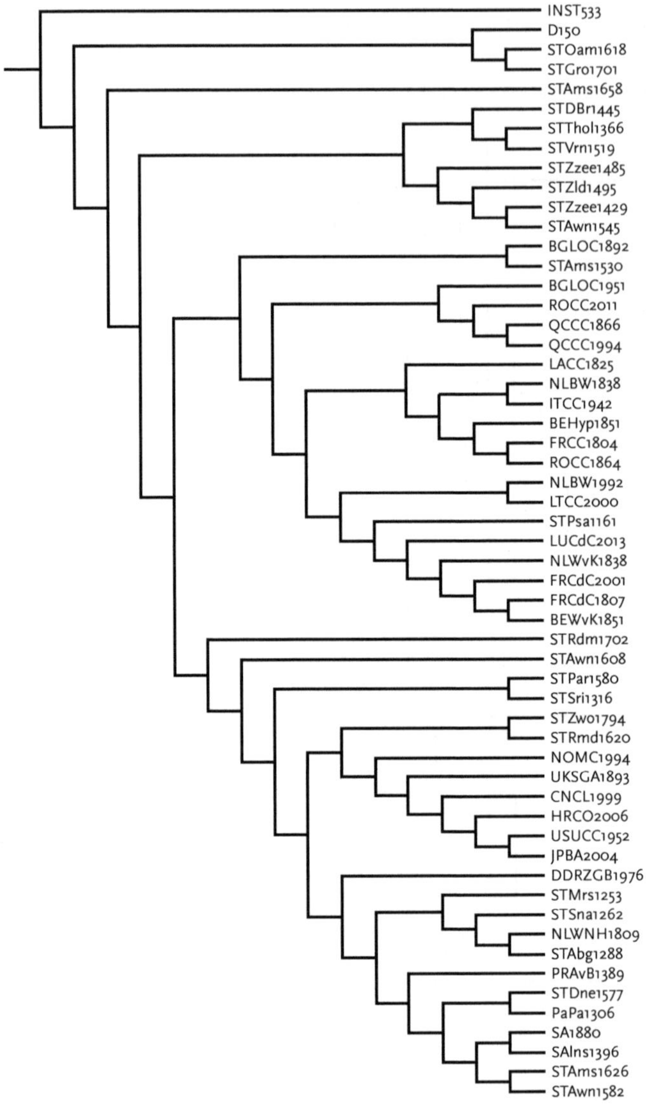

Figure 5.4 Unrooted majority rule consensus tree

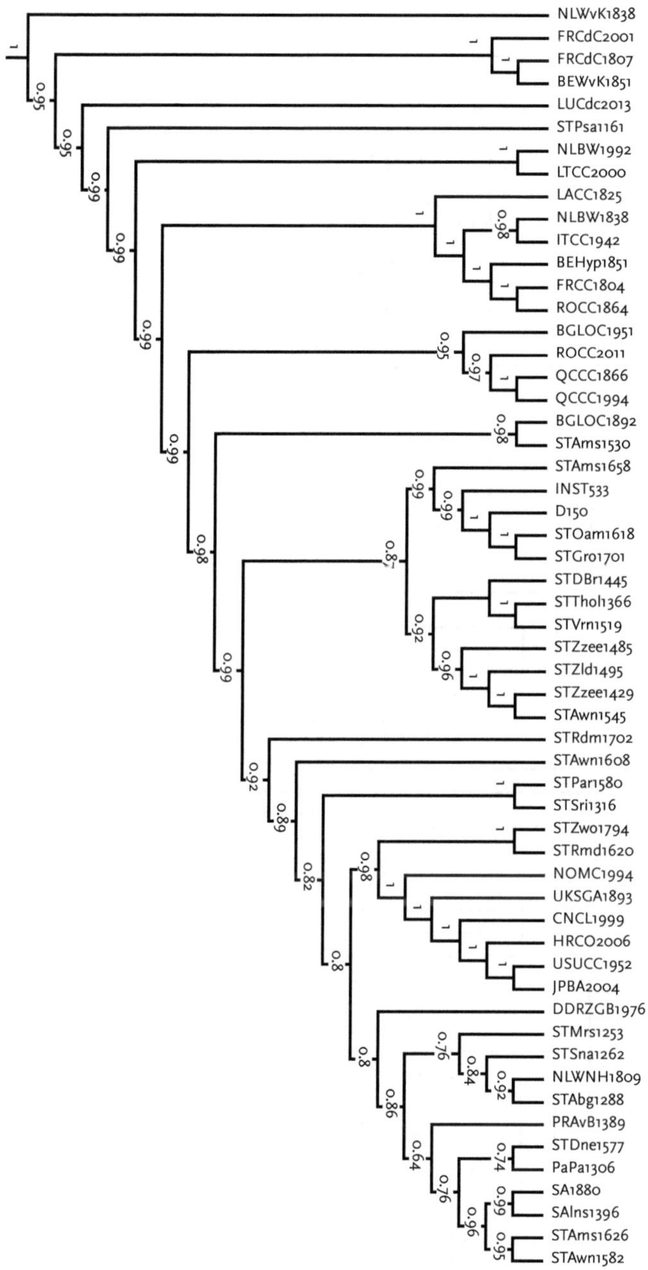

Figure 5.5 Majority rule consensus tree with Inst533 as outgroup

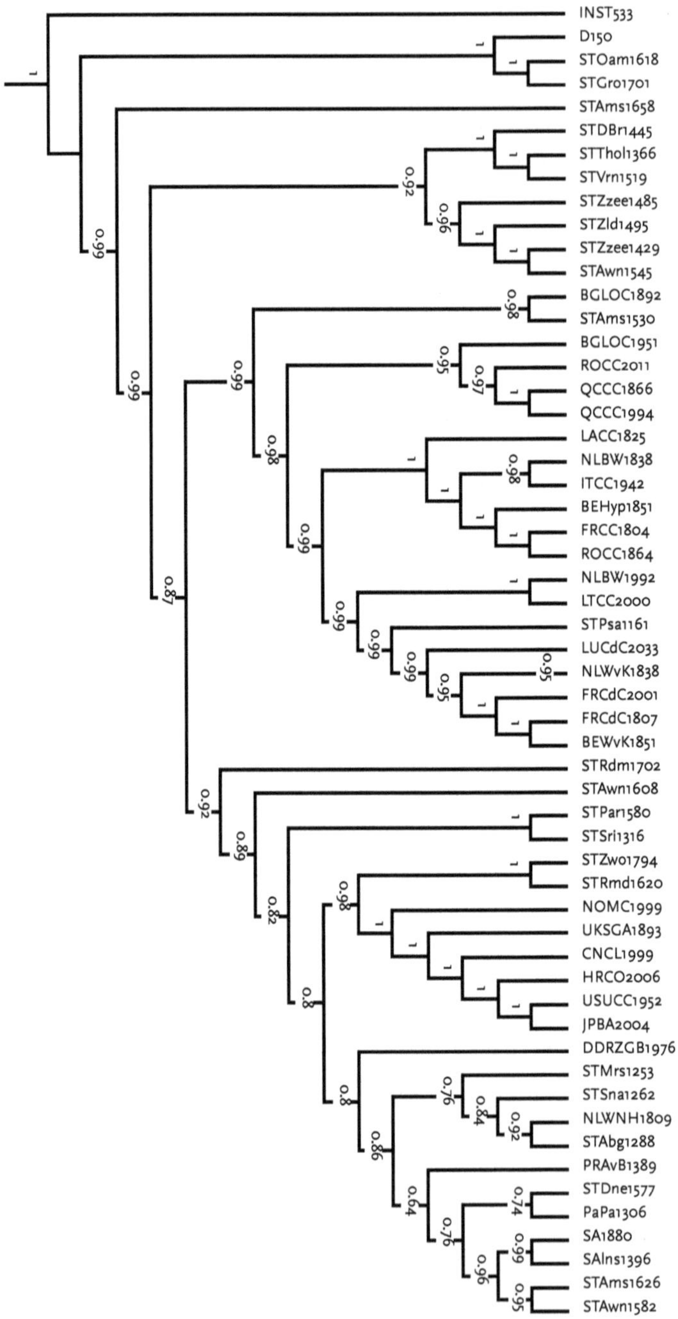

In each of these figures, the tree denotes the evolutionary relationships between the variations of the price payment rule. The ends of the branches stand for the 56 descendants, while the branch points (nodes) represent a point of divergence, at which one group splits into two descendant groups. The more recent the common ancestor, the more related the taxa. This means that descendants splitting from the same node can be considered as 'sisters', representing the closest possible relatives in the table. For example, in Figure 5.5, the *Coutume de Paris* of 1580 (STPar1580, no. 50) and the *Statuti di Sassari* of 1316 (STSri1316, no. 55) are represented as sisters, with their most recent common ancestor in the node immediately below (at the number '1'). Their next common ancestor is further below, at the lineage split at 0.82. The next common ancestor can be found at the split at 0.89. From this, it can be concluded that the provision in the customs of Antwerp of 1608 (STAwn1608, no. 48) is less related to STStri1316 than STPar1580.

Leaving aside the question of whether and how to root the trees, and whether Inst533 (no. 30) is the best possible outgroup to choose,[49] all four types of calculations return a comparable set of results. Although phylogenetic analysis can only hypothesize about the evolutionary ancestry of the variations, the trees provide a fresh perspective on the potential classification of the variations of the price payment rule. The majority rule consensus tree rooted in Inst533 (Figure 5.5) is in this respect exemplary. It shows a number of main clusters, which is even clearer if presented as a plotted diagram (Figure 5.6).

Figure 5.6 Majority rule consensus tree as plotted diagram

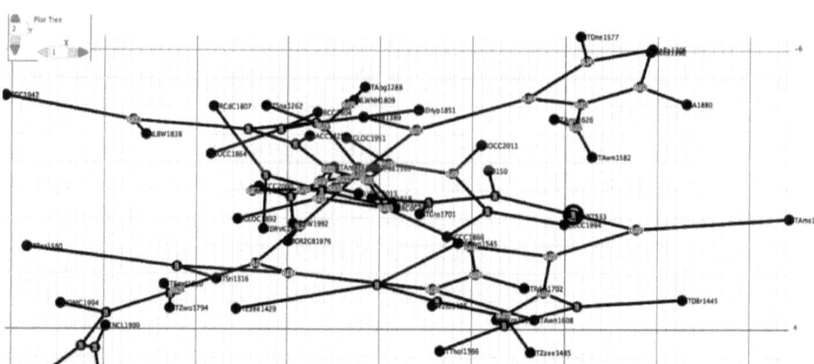

49 See for criticism on Tehrani for supposedly not choosing an outgroup: D. Morrison, 'The Phylogenetics of Little Red Riding Hood', The genealogical world of phylogenetic networks, blogspot http://phylonetworks.blogspot.be/2013/12/networks-trees-and-little-red-riding.html.

One cluster (clearly represented on the left side of Figure 5.6) is formed by provisions giving the seller of unpaid goods the right of 'stoppage in transitu' (NOMC 1994 (no. 18), UKSGA1893 (no. 19), CNCL1999 (no. 24), HRCO2006 (no. 17), USUCC1952 (no. 23) and JPBA2004 (no. 25)). These jurisdictions are genealogically quite apart from the Roman price payment rule as laid down in Inst533 (visible as the small black circle '1' on the right side of the diagram). This fits the historical explanation that seeks the provenance of stoppage in transit not in Roman sources, but either in medieval Italian statutes or in English common law.[50] Even though the French Commercial Code of 1807 only allows for reclaiming goods in transit in case of insolvency, the used algorithm apparently finds so many other differences that it does not place FRCdC1807 (no. 6), or BEWvK1851 (no. 9) for the same reason, in the same cluster. Historically, this is also the right approach: Art. 576 ff. of the French Commercial Code, written for merchants bringing a claim in case of insolvency of the buyer, was meant by the French legislator of 1807 to break with the previous law and is not linked to older sources.

Another cluster consists of STThol1366 (no. 32), STVrn1519 (no. 37), STZzee1485 (no. 34), STZld1495 (no. 36) and STZzee1429 (no. 33), flanked by STDbr1445 (no. 35) and STAwn1545 (no. 46) on either side. This cluster is genealogically much closer to Inst533. With the exception of the statute of Den Briel of 1445, all provisions seek the basis of recovery in retained ownership.[51] The rights also converge on a number of other points, including that they can be enforced both in and outside of the buyer's insolvency. The statute of Den Briel again diverges because it is only applicable to the reclaiming of sold wine and only in the case of credit. This does not prevent the algorithm to still place the statute in the same cluster as the other statutes from Zeeland. This seems the proper reconstruction; even though I am not aware of studies tracing the exact evolution of these statutes, their geographical proximity makes it likely they mutually influenced each other.

A third distinct type visible in Figures 5.5 and 5.6 is formed by LUCdC2013 (no. 10), NLWvK1838 (no. 3), FRCdC2001 (no. 7), FRCdC1807 (no. 6) and BEWvK1851 (no. 9). These are all provisions written for commercial relationships, though with varying requirements. They all lack an explicitly mentioned basis for the recovery. They also require insolvency of the buyer and deny the action to the seller in case the goods were already sold to a bona fide third party. The main difference is that the French and Belgian provisions require the goods to be in transit, while the Dutch and Luxembourg provisions also allow a claim in case the goods are already with the buyer. It is remarkable that Mesquite's algorithm indeed finds this inner relationship

50 Cf. Feenstra, *Reclame en revindicatie*, 207.

51 The coding of the statutes of Antwerp 1545 was based on the text of the statute that uses the term 'volghen.' This leads to an interpretation that is possibly contrary to the prevailing view among legal historians.

between the five provisions, all based on the example set by the French Commercial Code of 1807.

A fourth group can be found at the far right end of Figure 5.5, with varying degrees of genealogical proximity between STDne1577 (no. 49), PaPa1306 (no. 51) (the latter two being closely related), SA1880 (no. 26), SAIns1936 (no. 27), STAms1626 (no. 41) and STAwn 1582 (no. 47) (the latter two again being closely related). Except for the decision of the *Parlement de Paris* of 1306 (in which no basis is mentioned), they converge in seeking the basis for recovery in ownership. They diverge, among other things, in whether the claim can be brought both in and outside of the buyer's insolvency. The algorithm's reconstruction that these six provisions have one common ancestor is neither confirmed nor refuted in the literature.[52]

The calculation by Mesquite as apparent from Figure 5.5 reveals some more interesting connections. Apart from the eccentric similarity between the Dutch Civil Code of 1992 (NLBW1992, no. 4) and the Lithuanian Civil Code of 2000 (LTCC2000, no. 16), the local laws of the Oldambt in the province of Groningen (STOam1618, no. 38), of Groningen itself (STGr1701, no. 39) and the Digest (D150, no. 29) were coded almost entirely the same and therefore come out as having a common ancestor. If Inst533 had not been defined as the outgroup, it would have been in the same group. It cannot be derived from a phylogenetic analysis – blind to how evolution took place historically – that the law in Groningen is directly based on the Roman sources, but it does show the close similarities between these provisions.

Another interesting connection exists between the old Dutch Civil Code of 1838 (NLBW1838, no. 2) and the Italian Civil Code of 1942 (ITCC1942, no. 11). The two provisions in these codes were coded almost entirely similar, including the requirement that the action is only available if no credit was given to the buyer. This requirement is also found in both the original Roman sources and the old French and Dutch law. The main difference lies in the time within which to claim after delivery, with 30 days in Dutch law and 15 days in Italy. This difference in time limits (of which in total nine variations were identified in Annex 2) does not seem to affect the categorization by the Mesquite algorithm.

Phylogenetic analysis does not always lead to the same results as historical research. For example, there is little computational evidence for the influence of the statutes of Roermond by those of Antwerp.[53] However, the algorithm does place the local law of Zwolle (STZwo1794, no. 44) at the same genealogical level as the Roermond rule (STRmd1620, no. 45). Also, the presumed connection between the statutes of Genoa and Albenga (STAbg1288, no. 56) and the right of stoppage in transitu[54] does not show up in the diagram. The privilege of the Duke of Bavaria (PRAvB1389,

52 As based on Feenstra, *Reclame en revindicatie* and later writings.
53 Cf. Feenstra, *Reclame en revindicatie*, 140.
54 Cf. Feenstra, *Reclame en revindicatie*, 261 and Feenstra, *Ars Aequi* 55 (2006) 876.

no. 31), supposedly the oldest known instance of the seller's right to reclaim in the Netherlands,[55] remains a stand-alone provision. It would go too far to derive from this fact alone the conclusion that this privilege did not influence other Dutch provisions, but the lack of an immediate connection with any of the other texts is at least striking.

5.5 Conclusions

This chapter tests the potential of an alternative method to reconstruct the evolution of the unpaid seller's right to reclaim sold goods. Coding of the 56 variations of the price payment rule, and their subsequent examination with the help of Mesquite, reveals some of the possibilities computational phylogenetics has to offer. The most important finding is that phylogenetic methods can help to confirm or refute traditional classifications through which legal historians group the variations of the rule. The produced diagrams show alternatives for these traditional groupings.

This type of analysis can only hypothesize about the evolution of the price payment rule. However, this is not any different from traditional legal history. Both are dependent on the availability and interpretation of written texts. Moreover, phylogenetic analysis does not replace textual analysis but merely offers fresh insights on information that was previously not studied from a quantitative perspective. This does not mean phylogenetics offers a panacea for everything. For example, the analysis carried out in this chapter cannot confirm or refute Feenstra's assumption that the seller's right originated in medieval Italy (possibly in Pisa) and was then brought to France and further up North by merchants bringing along their own laws.[56] It also cannot solve the controversy over whether 17th-century Dutch law had Roman roots or already existed as an indigenous rule before the reception of Roman law.[57] It remains likely that the seller's right was already a part of French and Dutch customary laws from the 14th century onwards, at a time when influence of Roman law was unlikely. But the results so far are promising for a more elaborate use of phylogenetics that could also open doors to reconstructing the origins of the provisions, their history and possibly even the rate at which changes happened. If in biology phylogenetics is able to produce such results in studying species, it must be possible to do the same for written texts.

55 Cf. Feenstra, id., 178.
56 Feenstra, id., 255.
57 Feenstra, id., 154.

Annex 1 Full list of texts

1. *NLWNH1809*

Wetboek Napoleon ingerigt voor het Koningrijk Holland 1809 (Netherlands)
Art. 1839: 'Zoo lang de koopprijs van gekochte en geleverde meubelen niet betaald is, en die meubelen in natura in eenen insolventen boedel voorhanden zijn, heeft de verkooper regt van reclame op dezelve; (...)

Door het bij dit artikel bepaalde wordt geene verandering gemaakt in de wetten en gebruiken der commercie omtrent de reclamen.'

2. *NLBW1838*

Burgerlijk Wetboek 1838 (Netherlands)
Art. 1191: '1. Indien de verkoop zonder tijdsbepaling is gedaan, heeft de verkooper zelfs de bevoegdheid om de goederen terug te eischen, zoo lang deze zich in handen van den kooper bevinden, en het weder-verkoopen daarvan te beletten, mits de terugeisching geschiede binnen dertig dagen na de aflevering. (...)'

Art. 1192a BW (introduced 1935): '1. Het regt van den verkooper vervalt, indien de goederen na zich in het bezit van den oorspronkelijken kooper of van iemand van zijnentwege te hebben bevonden, door eenen derde te goeder trouw zijn gekocht en aan dezelven afgeleverd.

2. In geval echter de koopprijs nog niet door dien derde betaald is, kan de oorspronkelijke verkooper de gelden tot aan het beloop zijner rekening voor zich vorderen, mits de vordering geschiede binnen den tijd van dertig dagen na de oorspronkelijke aflevering.'

3. *NLWvK1838*

Wetboek van Koophandel 1838 (Netherlands)
Art. 230: 'In geval koopmanschappen zijn verkocht en geleverd, en de koopprijs niet ten volle is gekweten, is de verkooper, bij faillissement van den kooper, geregtigd om de koopmanschappen terug te vorderen, onder de volgende bepalingen.'

Art. 231: 'Tot de uitoefening van het regt van terugvordering wordt vereischt dat de koopmanschappen, zonder vermenging met andere, dezelfde zijn welke zijn verkocht en geleverd. (...)'

Art. 232: 'Koopmanschappen, hetzij op tijd, hetzij zonder tijdsbepaling, verkocht, kunnen worden terug gevorderd, indien dezelve nog onderweg zijn, hetzij te land, hetzij te water, of indien dezelve zich nog in natura bevinden onder den failliet, of onder eenen derde, die de koopmanschappen voor hem bezit of bewaart.

In beide gevallen, kan deze terugvordering slechts worden gedaan binnen den tijd van dertig dagen, te rekenen van den dag, waarop de koopmanschappen onder den failliet of onder den derde zijn opgeslagen.'

Art. 237: 'Indien de teruggevorderde koopmanschappen door eenen derde, te goeder trouw, zijn in beleening genomen, behoudt de verkooper zijn regt van terugvordering, maar is, daarentegen, verpligt aan den geldschieter te voldoen het bedrag van het daarop geschoten geld, met de verschuldigde interessen en kosten.'

Art. 238: 'De terugvordering der koopmanschappen vervalt, indien dezelve, gedurende de reis, op facturen en op cognossementen of vrachtbrieven te goeder trouw door eenen derde zijn gekocht.

Niettemin is de oorspronkelijke verkooper, in dat geval, bevoegd den koopprijs, zoo lang dezelve nog niet is gekweten, tot het beloop zijner inschuld, bij den kooper in te vorderen, en hij is bevoorregt op die penningen, zonder dat dezelve met den boedel van den failliet mogen worden vermengd.

De bepalingen van het vorige lid zijn ook toepasselijk op het geval dat de koopmanschappen, na zich in het bezit van den failliet, of van iemand van zijnentwege, te hebben bevonden, door koop en levering, te goeder trouw, de eigendom van eenen derde zijn geworden.'

4. *NLBW1992*

Burgerlijk Wetboek 1992 (Netherlands)

Art. 7:39: 'De verkoper van een roerende, aan de koper afgeleverde zaak die niet een registergoed is, kan, indien de prijs niet betaald is en in verband daarmee aan de vereisten voor een ontbinding als bedoeld in artikel 265 van Boek 6 is voldaan, de zaak door een tot de koper gerichte schriftelijke verklaring terugvorderen. Door deze verklaring wordt de koop ontbonden en eindigt het recht van de koper of zijn rechtsverkrijger; (...).'

Art. 7:41: 'De bevoegdheid tot terugvordering kan slechts worden uitgeoefend voor zover het afgeleverde zich nog in dezelfde staat bevindt als waarin het werd afgeleverd.'

Art. 7:42: '1. Tenzij de zaak in handen van de koper is gebleven, vervalt de bevoegdheid tot terugvordering wanneer de zaak overeenkomstig artikel 90 lid 1 of artikel 91 van Boek 3 anders dan om niet is overgedragen aan een derde die redelijkerwijs niet behoefde te verwachten dat het recht zou worden uitgeoefend. (...)'

Art. 7:44: 'De in artikel 39 omschreven bevoegdheid van de verkoper vervalt, wanneer zowel zes weken zijn verstreken nadat de vordering tot betaling van de koopprijs opeisbaar is geworden, als zestig dagen, te rekenen van de dag waarop de zaak onder de koper of onder iemand van zijnentwege is opgeslagen.'

5. *FRCC1804*

Code Civil 1804 (France)

Art. 2102-4 (since 2006 Art. 2332-4 CC): 'Les créances privilégiees sur certains meubles sont: (...) 4. Le prix d'effets mobiliers non payés, s'ils sont encore en la possession du débiteur, soit qu'il ait acheté à terme ou sans terme; Si la vente a été faite sans terme, le vendeur peut meme revendiquer ces effets tant qu'ils sont en la possession de l'acheteur, et en empecher la revente, pourvu que la revendication soit faite dans la huitaine de la livraison, et que les effets se trouvent dans le meme état dans lequel cette livraison a été faite.'

6. *FRCdC1807*

Code de Commerce 1807 (France)

Art. 576: 'Le vendeur pourra, en cas de faillite, revendiquer les marchandises par lui vendues et livrées, et dont le prix ne lui a pas été payé, dans les cas et aux conditions ci-après exprimés.'

Art. 577: 'La revendication ne pourra avoir lieu que pendant les marchandises expédiées seront encore en route, soit par terre, soit par eau, et avant qu'elles oient entrées dans les magasins du failli ou dans les magasins du commissionnaire chargé de les vendre pour le compte du failli.'

Art. 578: 'Elles ne pourront etre revendiquees, si, avant leur arrivee, elles ont ete vendues sans fraude, sur factures et connaissements ou lettres de voiture.'

7. *FRCdC2001*

Code de Commerce 2001 (France)

Art. L624-9: 'La revendication des meubles ne peut être exercée que dans le délai de trois mois suivant la publication du jugement ouvrant la procédure.'

Art. L624-11: 'Le privilège et le droit de revendication établis par le 4° de l'article 2332 du code civil au profit du vendeur de meubles ainsi que l'action résolutoire ne peuvent être exercés que dans la limite des dispositions des articles L. 624-12 à L. 624-18 du présent code.'

Art. L624-12: 'Peuvent être revendiquées, si elles existent en nature, en tout ou partie, les marchandises dont la vente a été résolue antérieurement au jugement ouvrant la procédure soit par décision de justice, soit par le jeu d'une condition résolutoire acquise. (...)'

Art. L624-13: 'Peuvent être revendiquées les marchandises expédiées au débiteur tant que la tradition n'en a point été effectuée dans ses magasins ou dans ceux du commissionnaire chargé de les vendre pour son compte.'

Néanmoins, la revendication n'est pas recevable si, avant leur arrivée, les marchandises ont été revendues sans fraude, sur factures ou titres de transport réguliers.'

Art. L624-16: 'Peuvent être revendiqués, à condition qu'ils se retrouvent en nature, les biens meubles remis à titre précaire au débiteur ou ceux transférés dans un patrimoine fiduciaire dont le débiteur conserve l'usage ou la jouissance en qualité de constituant. (...)'

8. BEHyp1851

Hypotheekwet/Loi hypothécaire 1851 (Belgium)
Art. 20 (5): 'Indien de verkoop zonder tijdsbepaling gedaan is, kan de verkoper de verkochte voorwerpen zelfs terugvorderen zolang zij zich in het bezit van de koper bevinden, en de wederverkoop ervan beletten, mits de terugvordering geschiedt binnen acht dagen na de levering en de voorwerpen zich nog in dezelfde staat bevinden als ten tijde van de levering.' / 'Si la vente a été faite sans terme, le vendeur peut même revendiquer les objets vendus tant qu'ils sont en la possession de l'acheteur, et en empêcher la revente, pourvu que la revendication soit faite dans la huitaine de la livraison et qu'ils se trouvent dans le même état que lors de la livraison.'

9. BEWvK1851

Wetboek van Koophandel/Code de Commerce 1851 (Belgium)
Art. 568 (now Art. 104 Faillissementswet/Loi sur les Faillites 1997): 'Kunnen ook worden teruggevorderd de aan de gefailleerde verzonden koopwaren, zolang de overgave ervan niet is geschied in zijn magazijnen of in deze van de commissionair die gelast is ze te verkopen voor rekening van de gefailleerde.

De terugvordering is niettemin niet ontvankelijk wanneer de koopwaren, voor hun aankomst, zonder bedrog zijn verkocht (...)'

10. LUCdC2013

Code de Commerce 2013 (Luxembourg)
Art. 566: 'Pourront être revendiquées en cas de faillite, les remises en effets de commerce ou autres titres non encore payés, et qui se trouveront en nature dans le portefeuille du failli à la date du jugement déclaratif de la faillite, lorsque ces remises auront été faites par le propriétaire avec simple mandat d'en faire le recouvrement et d'en garder la valeur à sa disposition, ou lorsqu'elles auront été de sa part spécialement affectées à des paiements déterminés.'

Art. 567: 'Les biens meubles corporels non fongibles consignés au failli, soit à titre de dépôt, soit pour être vendus pour le compte du propriétaire, peuvent être revendiqués, à condition qu'ils se trouvent en nature au moment de l'ouverture de la procédure.

Les biens meubles incorporels non fongibles en possession du failli ou détenus par lui peuvent être revendiqués par celui qui les a confiés au failli ou par leur propriétaire, à condition qu'ils soient séparables de tous autres biens meubles incorporels non fongibles au moment de l'ouverture de la procédure, les frais afférents étant à charge du revendiquant.'

Art. 568: 'Pourront aussi être revendiquées les marchandises expédiées au failli, tant que la tradition n'en aura point été effectuée dans ses magasins, ou dans ceux du commissionnaire chargé de les vendre pour le compte du failli.

Néanmoins, la revendication ne sera pas recevable, si, avant leur arrivée, les marchandises ont été vendues sans fraude, sur factures et sur connaissements ou lettres de voitures signés par l'expéditeur.'

11. ITCC1942

Codice Civile 1942 (Italy)
Art. 1519: 'Se la vendita stata fatta senza dilazione per il pagamento del prezzo, il venditore, in mancanza di pagamento, pu riprendere il possesso delle cose vendute, finch queste si trovano presso il compratore (1156), purch la domanda sia proposta entro quindici giorni dalla consegna e le cose si trovino nello stato in cui erano al tempo della consegna stessa.' (…)

12. ROCC1864

Codul Civil 1864 (Romania)
Art. 1730: 'Creanţele privilegiate asupra oricăror mobile sunt: (...)

5. Preţul pentru lucruri mobile neplătite, dacă se afla încă în posesiunea debitorului, chiar şi în cazul când a cumpărat cu termen de plată. Dacă vânzarea sa făcut fără termen de plată, vânzătorul poate chiar s-a revendice obiectele vândute, pe cat timp se afla în posesiunea cumpărătorului, şi poate să împiedice revinderea acelor lucruri, dacă însă s-a făcut cererea sa în termen de opt zile după trădarea lucrurilor, şi dacă lucrurile se afla încă tot în starea în care se găseau la timpul trădării lor.'

13. ROCC2011

Codul Civil 2011 (Romania)
Art. 1727: '(Restituirea bunului mobil): 1. Atunci când vânzarea s-a făcut fără termen de plată, iar cumpărătorul nu a plătit preţul, vânzătorul poate ca, în cel mult 15 zile de la data predării, să declare rezoluţiunea fără punere în întârziere şi să ceară restituirea bunului mobil vândut, cât timp bunul este încă în posesia cumpărătorului şi nu a suferit transformări.

2. În cazul prevăzut la alin. (1), dacă acţiunea în restituire nu a fost introdusă în condiţiile stabilite de acesta, vânzătorul nu mai poate opune celorlalţi creditori ai cumpărătorului efectele rezoluţiunii ulterioare a contractului pentru neplata preţului. Dispoziţiile Art. 1.648 sau ale Art. 1.649, după caz, rămân aplicabile.'

14. BGLOC1892

Закон за задълженията и договорите (Law of Obligations and Contracts 1892 (Bulgaria))

Чл. 282: 'Когато се касае за движими имущества, развалянето на продажбата става по право в интереса на продавача, ако купувачът не се е явил да получи вещта, преди да е изтекъл определения за продаването й срок, или като се е явил да я получи, не е предложил в същото време нейната цена, освен ако е бил условен един по-дълъг срок за плащането на цената.'

15. BGLOC1951

Закон за задълженията и договорите (Law of Obligations and Contracts 1951 (Bulgaria))

Чл. 202: 'Когато не е даден срок за плащането на цената и купувачът получи вещта, без да плати, продавачът може да иска да му се върне вещта в 15-дневен срок от предаването, ако тя се намира още у купувача и е в състоянието, в което е била предадена.

Това право не може да се упражни във вреда на кредиторите на купувача, наложили запор върху вещта или получили същата в залог, без да знаят, че цената не е платена.'

16. LTCC2000

Civilinis Kodeksas 2000 (Lithuania)

Art. 6.345: 'straipsnis. Pirkėjo pareigos sumokėti kainą neįvykdymo teisinės pasekmės

1. Jeigu kilnojamieji daiktai jau perduoti pirkėjui, o jis kainos nesumokėjo, pardavėjas turi teisę atsisakyti sutarties raštu apie tai pranešdamas pirkėjui ir išreikalauti daiktus iš pirkėjo. Jeigu nesumokėta tik kainos dalis, pardavėjas gali išreikalauti tik nesumokėtą daikto kainos dalį, kai daiktas yra dalusis. Išreikalavimo teisę pardavėjas turi iki tol, kol daiktai dar yra jų perdavimo vietos valstybėje arba kol jie nėra atlygintinai perleisti trečiajam asmeniui, nėra įkeisti ar jiems nenustatyta uzufrukto teisė.

2. Kai pirkėjas tampa nemokus, pardavėjas negali išreikalauti daiktų, už kuriuos nesumokėta, jeigu per protingą terminą pirkėjo administratorius pasiūlo sumokėti kainą ar pateikia šios prievolės įvykdymo užtikrinimą.

3. Visais kitais šio straipsnio 1 ir 2 dalyse nenurodytais atvejais atsiranda šio kodekso 6.314 straipsnyje numatytos teisinės pasekmės.'

17. HRCO2006

Zakon o obveznim odnosima (Civil Obligations Act) 2006 (Croatia)

Art. 398: 'Delay of Delivery in Cases Where the Thing is Carried

(1) Kad se predaja stvari ostvaruje uručenjem prijevozniku, prodavatelj može odgoditi odašiljanje stvari do isplate cijene, ili poslati stvar tako da zadrži pravo raspolaganja njome za vrijeme prijevoza.

(2) Ako je zadržao pravo raspolaganja stvarju za vrijeme prijevoza, prodavatelj može zahtijevati da stvar ne bude predana kupcu u odredišnom mjestu dok ne isplati cijenu, a kupac nije dužan isplatiti cijenu prije nego što je imao mogućnost pregledati stvar.

(3) Međutim, kad ugovor predviđa plaćanje uz predaju odgovarajuće isprave, kupac nema pravo odbiti isplatu cijene zbog toga što nije imao mogućnost pregledati stvar.'

18. NOMC1994

Lov om sjøfarten (Maritime Code) 1994 (Norway)

§ 307: 'Stansningsrett.

Den rett en selger har ved mislighold til å hindre utlevering av godset til kjøperen eller dennes bo eller til å kreve det tilbake, gjelder selv om konnossementet er overlevert til kjøperen.

Stansningsretten kan ikke gjøres gjeldende overfor en tredjeperson som i god tro har ervervet et ordre- eller ihendehaverkonnossement.'

19. UKSGA1893

Sale of Goods Act 1893 (United Kingdom)

S. 44: 'Subject tot the provisions of this Act, when the buyer of goods becomes insolvent, the unpaid seller who has parted with the possession of the goods has the right of stopping them in transitu, that is to say, he may resume possession of the goods as long as they are in course of transit, and may retain them until payment or tender of the price.'

20. QCCC1866

Code Civil du Bas Canada (Civil Code of Lower Canada) 1866

Art. 1998: 'The unpaid vendor of a thing has two privileged rights: 1. A right to revendicate it; 2. A right of preference upon its price. In the case of insolvent traders, these rights must be exercised within fifteen days after the sale.'

Art. 1999: 'The right to revendicate is subject to four conditions:

1. The sale must not have been made on credit;

2. The things must still be entire and in the same condition;

3. The thing must not have passed into the hands of a third party who has paid for it;

4. It must be exercised within eight days after the delivery; saving the provision concerning insolvent traders contained in the last preceding article.

/ Le vendeur d'une chose non payée peut exercer deux droits privilégiés:

1. Celui de revendiquer la chose ;

2. Celui d'être préféré sur le prix.

Dans les cas de faillite, ces droits ne peuvent être exercés que dans les quinze jours qui suivent la vente.

1999. Pour exercer cette revendication quatre conditions sont requises:

1 . Que la vente ait été faite sans terme;

2. Que la chose soit encore entière et dans le même état;

3. Qu'elle ne soit pas passée entre les mains d'un tiers qui en ait payé le prix;

4. Que la revendication soit exercée dans les huit jours de la livraison; sauf la disposition relative à la faillite et contenue en l'article qui précède.'

21. QCCC1994

Code Civil du Québec 1994

Art. 1741: 'Where the sale of movable property was made without a term, the seller may, within 30 days of delivery, consider the sale resolved and revendicate the property if the buyer, being in default, has failed to pay the price and the property is still entire and in the same condition, not having passed into the hands of a third person who has paid the price thereof or of a hypothecary creditor who has obtained surrender thereof.

Where the buyer is in default for failing to pay the price and the property meets the conditions prescribed for resolution of the sale, the seizure of the property by a third person is no hindrance to the rights of the seller.

/ Lorsque la vente d'un bien meuble a été faite sans terme, le vendeur peut, dans les 30 jours de la délivrance, considérer la vente comme résolue et revendiquer le bien, si l'acheteur, alors qu'il est en demeure, fait défaut de payer le prix et si le meuble est encore entier et dans le même état, sans être passé entre les mains d'un tiers qui en a payé le prix ou d'un créancier hypothécaire qui a obtenu le délaissement du bien.

La saisie par un tiers, alors que l'acheteur est en demeure de payer le prix et que le bien est dans les conditions prescrites pour la résolution, ne fait pas obstacle au droit du vendeur.'

22. LACC1825

Civil Code of Louisiana 1825

Art. 3196 (now Art. 3229): 'Vendor's claim for restitution.

If the sale was not made on credit, the seller may even claim back the things in kind, which were thus sold, as long as they are in possession of the purchaser, and prevent the resale of them; provided the claim for restitution be made within eight days of the delivery at farthest, and that the identity of the objects be established.'

Art. 3197 (now Art. 3230): 'When the things reclaimed consist in merchandise, which is sold in bales, packages or cases, the claim shall not be admitted if they have been untied, unpacked or taken out of the cases and mixed with other things of the same nature belonging to the purchaser, so that their identity can no longer be established.'

Art. 3198: 'But if the things sold are of such a nature as to be easily recognized, as household furniture, even although the papers or cloths, which covered them at the time of delivery, be removed, the claim for restitution shall be allowed.'

Art. 3230: 'When the things reclaimed consist in merchandise, which is sold in bales, packages or cases, the claim shall not be admitted if they have been untied, unpacked or taken out of the cases and mixed with other things of the same nature belonging to the purchaser, so that their identity can no longer be established.'

Art. 3231: 'But if the things sold are of such a nature as to be easily recognized, as household furniture, even although the papers or cloths, which covered them at the time of delivery, be removed, the claim for restitution shall be allowed.'

23. USUCC1952

Uniform Commercial Code (NCCUSL/ALI) 1952

§ 2-705: 'Seller's Stoppage of Delivery in Transit or Otherwise.

(1) The seller may stop delivery of goods in the possession of a carrier or other bailee when he discovers the buyer to be insolvent (Section 2-702) and may stop delivery of carload, truckload, planeload or larger shipments of express or freight when the buyer repudiates or fails to make a payment due before delivery or if for any other reason the seller has a right to withhold or reclaim the goods.

(2) As against such buyer the seller may stop delivery until

(a) receipt of the goods by the buyer; or

(b) acknowledgment to the buyer by any bailee of the goods except a carrier that the bailee holds the goods for the buyer; or

(c) such acknowledgment to the buyer by a carrier by reshipment or as warehouseman; or

(d) negotiation to the buyer of any negotiable document of title covering the goods.

(3)(a) To stop delivery the seller must so notify as to enable the bailee by reasonable diligence to prevent delivery of the goods.

(b) After such notification the bailee must hold and deliver the goods according to the directions of the seller but the seller is liable to the bailee for any ensuing charges or damages.

(c) If a negotiable document of title has been issued for goods the bailee is not obliged to obey a notification to stop until surrender of the document.

(d) A carrier who has issued a non-negotiable bill of lading is not obliged to obey a notification to stop received from a person other than the consignor.'

24. CNCL1999

Contract Law of the People's Republic of China 1999

Art. 308: 'Prior to carrier's delivery of the cargo to the consignee, the consignor may require the carrier to suspend the carriage, return the cargo, change the destination or deliver the cargo to another consignee, provided that it shall indemnify the carrier for any loss it sustains as a result.'

25. JPBA2004

Bankruptcy Act 2004 (Japan)

Art. 63 (1): 'Where the seller has dispatched the goods that are the subject of sale to the buyer, in case an order of commencement of bankruptcy proceedings is made against the buyer while the buyer has not yet paid the price in full and not yet received the goods at the destination, the seller may segregate the goods; provided, however, this shall not preclude a bankruptcy trustee from requesting the delivery thereto of the goods by paying the price in full.'

26. SA1880 (South Africa)

Daniels v Cooper, EDC I, 174 (1880); Laing v South African Mining Co Ltd, 1921 AD 387, 399

27. SAIns1936

Insolvency Act 1936 (South Africa)

S. 36(1): 'If a person, before the sequestration of his estate, by virtue of a contract of purchase and sale which provided for the payment of the purchase price upon delivery of the property in question to the purchaser, received any movable property without paying the purchase price in full, the seller may, after the sequestration of the purchaser's estate, reclaim that property if within ten days after delivery thereof he has given notice in writing to the purchaser or to the trustee of the purchaser's insolvent estate or to the Master, that he reclaims the property.'

28. DDRZGB1976

Zivilgesetzbuch der Deutschen Demokratischen Republik 1976
§ 139 (3): 'Das Eigentum geht mit Übergabe der Ware und Zahlung des Kaufpreises auf den Käufer über, soweit nichts anderes vereinbart ist.'

29. D150

Digest 150 (Pomponius)
18.1.19: 'Quod vendidi non aliter fit accipientis quam si aut pretium nobis solutum sit aut satis eo nomine factum vel etiam fidem habuerimus emptori sine ulla satisfactione.'

30. Inst533

Institutes of Justinian 533
2.1.41: 'Sed si qu idem ex causa donationis aut dotis aut qualibet alia ex causa tradantur, sine dubio transferuntur: venditae vero et traditiae non aliter emptori adquiruntur, quam si is venditori pretium solverit vel alio modo ei satisfecerit, veluti expromissore aut pignore dato. Quod cavetur quidem etiam lege duodecim tabularum: tamen recte dicitur et iure gentium, id est iure naturali, id effici, sed si is qui vendidit fidem emptoris secutus fuerit, dicendum est statim rem emptoris fieri.'

31. PRAvB1389

Privilege of Albert, Duke of Bavaria 7 May 1389 (Feenstra 1949, 178)
'...Item waert so, dat enich van den coepluyden voerseyd vercofte goet binnen onsen lande ende heerscappien voerseyd ende die copere van den goede worde voervluchtig, eer hiit betaelt hadde, dat dan die voerseide vercoper syn goede volghen mach; ende wair hu sijn goet vinden mach bi goeden bewisinghe of mit sinen mercke goet doen mach, dattet syn goet gheweest hebben, so sal men den voerseyden vercopere syn goed weder telivereren, waer dat mens vint, sonder voert te vervolghene...'

32. STThol1366

Handvest Tholen 1366 (Van Mieris, Groot Charterboek III, 202)
Art. 41: 'Item, want dicwyle stoot gevalt onder die coeplude inder betalinghe van alrehande dagelyxe comenscap, die men coept, ende vercoept om gereet gelt, soe wetten wy, ende geven onsen lieden, soe wanneer die vercoper, hy sy van buten, of van binnen, syn comenscap, die hy om gereet gelt vercoept, ghelevert heeft, ende syn gelt daer of niet ontfaen, soe mach hy des ander daghes, of des derdes dages comen an den Balyu, ende gerens rechts, soe sal die Balyu rechte voert metten Scepenen

gaen metten vercoper, ende doen hem geldinge aen des copers lieflixte goet anderhalf scatte in eygendomme, mar dat mach die coper werder lossen by der sonnen met enen scatte gelde, of die pande verloren…'

33. STZzee1429

Keur Zierikzee 1429 (Werken OVR II, 9 (1908), 133)
Art. 48: 'Item soe wie syn goed vercoopt om ghereedt geld, ygerlic besie hem selven wel, laet hy syn goed van hem draghen onbetaelt, hy en volget sonder merren sinen goede na om tgelt...'

34. STZzee1485

Keur Zierikzee 1485 (Werken OVR II, 9 (1908), 254)
Art. 69: 'Item soe wye zyn goet vercoopt om gereet gelt, ygerlijck voirzie hemselven wel, laet hy zijn goet van hem dragen onbetaelt, hy en volget binnen den seven dage nae om dat weder te anvaerden, behouden voirt zijns rechts, off somme zijn gelt te hebben ende dat mit rechte…'

35. STDBr1445

Keur Den Briel 1445 (Werken OVR II, 2 (1901), 127)
Art. 18: 'Item nyemant en sal wijn doen halen, tenzij mit reden gelde. Ende ware tsake, dat yemant sonder ghereedt gelt wijn uutborchde, dat wait den vercoper ende denghenen, die den wijn te borghe dede halen, huerlijc op een boete van XX sc. Hollants, also dicke als yemant hiermede bevonden worde, rechtevoort off te panden, halff mijn here ende die ander helfft die stede.'

36. STZld1495

Keur Zeeland 1495 (Keuren van Zeeland, ed. Fruin, Werken OVR II, 20 (1920), 219)
Cap. II, Art. 34: 'Item, dat zoe wie eenich goet coopt omme gereedt ghelt, ende hy dat goet wech voerdt sonder betalen, die vercooper sal binnen der voorsschen dat goet mogen doen bestellen bij scout ende scepenen van de plecken, daer hijt vinden sal, ende tzyne daeran ende an den cooper verhalen.'

37. STVrn1519

Keur Voorne 1519 (Keuren ende Privilegien van Voorne, Rotterdam 1717, 85)
Art. 51: 'Iten als yemandt eenich goed koopt met ghereden ghelde ende dat wech voert eer hy betaelt heeft, oft des verkoopers ghemoede ghehadt heeft, soos al die verkoper dat moghen vervolghen ende aenvaerden tot allen plecken daer hy dat vinden

zal, ende sal die ghene die dat alsoo wechgevoert heeft, verbeuren tegens den Heere 's sestig Ponden swarten, ende partyen repareren van haer schade.'

38. STOam1618

Landregt der beyden Oldambten 1618, IV (Groningen 1650, 109)
Art. 91: 'Als eenigh goedt verkogt ende gelevert werdt, soo werdt nochtans de koper daer van geen heer, voor ende al-eer 't selve goedt betaelt is, ten waer de verkoper vertrouwde, ofte door obligatie ofte anders gecontenteert was.'

39. STGro1701

Groninger Ordonnantie op allerhande conventiën en contracten 25 April 1701 (Corpus der Groninger regten, 1725, II, no. 18)
Van koop ende verkoop, Art. 3: 'Het verkogte goed nochtans, wordt den kooper eerst eygen, als de bedongene koop-penningen zijn voldaen, alwaer het oock dat de over-levering daer op was geschiet, soo dat de verkooper sijn eigendom behoudt, tot dat de prijs is betaelt, ten sij dat het verkochte goedt waer vertrouwt of op tijdt verkogt, ende de verkooper het credit van den kooper hadde gevolgt.'

40. STAms1530

Keur Amsterdam 5 February 1530 (Noordkerk, Handvesten (...) der stad Amstelredam 1748, 2, 502)
'dat soo wanneer imant eenige 't zy eetbaer ofte andere waren ofte goederen gekocht heeft met gereeden gelde ende de verkooper onraet vernemende van quade betalinge, alsdan de verkooper wel geraeckt sal wesen aen die selve verkochte waren ofte goeden die hij weder tot hem sal mogen nemen in allen schijne of die onverkocht hadden geweest.'

41. STAms1626

Keur van Amsterdam 14 October 1626 (Noordkerk, Handvesten 1748, 2, 504)
'als een koopman verkocht heeft eenige goederen op twaelf maenden, mits rabatter-ende, ende dezelve goederen gelevert hebbende, daer na den kooper komt insolvent te worden ofte in gebreke blijft te betalen, alsdan de verkooper niet en vermagh ende vrij staet sijne vercochte ende geleverde goederen te vervolgen, ende die achterhalende te aenvaerden ende naer hem te nemen, sonder dat hy verkooper wegen alsulken schult gehouden is in concurrentie te komen.'

42. STAms1658

Keur Amsterdam 31 January 1658 (Noordkerk, Handvesten 1748, 2, 503)
'dat van nu voortaen alle die gene, die hare koopmanschappen, goederen ende waren om contant verkoopen, zullen gehouden sijn de betalinge der zelver te vorderen binnen den tijt van zes weken na de koop en leverantie; ende by aldien zo die niet konnen bekomen, zullen zo de respective koopers op den eersten recht-dagh na de zes weken in rechte moeten betrecken: ende by manquement van dien, vervallen van 't recht van preferentie, ende hare goederen niet vermogen te vindiceren, maer gehouden werden, als of op de selve op tijt hadden verkogt (...).'

43. STRdm1702

Generale Keure ende ordonnantie der stad Rotterdam, Vol. II, 1712, p. 263
'Alle degene die eenige goederen om contant hebben verkocht, warden verstaen den eigendom te behouden, en zulks het recht om dezelve goederen te kunnen revindiceren, uit handen niet alleen van de coopers maer ook van derde possesseurs, ter tijdt tot de koop-penningen effectivelijk zullen zijn voldaan.'

44. STZwo1794

Stadrecht Zwolle 1794 (Zwolle 1794, p. 303)
Art. III.12.3: Art. 3: 'Als er geen tijd van betaalinge en overgave der verkochte goederen gesteld is, zal die tijd zijn terstond na de geslooten koop.'

Art. 4: 'Doch ten aanzien van waren, die door kooplieden in 't gros zijn verkocht, zal, als er geen beding ter contrair gemaakt is, voor prompte betaaling gehouden worden de zesweekste dag na de leverantie.'

Art. 5: 'Kwam des koopers crediet binnen desen tijd van zes weeken te verminderen, zoo heeft de verkooper het recht van reclame op die verkochte waaren zooverre die onder den kooper nog worden bevonden, ofte onder een derden, die dezelve niet contant noch ter goede trouwe betaald heeft, als ook zoo verre die derde een gedeelte van den prijs daarop betaald heeft, mits de reclamant het uitgeschooten geld terig geeft.'

45. STRmd1620

Landt en Stadtrechten in 't Overquartier van Roermond III, 2.2.1 (Berkvens et al, Geldrische Land- en Stadsrechten in het overkwartier Roermond, 2, 144)
Art. 1: 'Al is 't dat men syn eigen goet heeft verkocht, ofte anderssints verhandelt ende opgedragen, oft gelevert, soo wanneer men nochtans daer van niet en is betaelt oft voldaen, ende dat het selve noch onverhandtplicht oft ongelevert is in de handen van de cooper, oft tot syn gebiede ende beveel noch staet, soo magh men daer op syn

vervolgh doen, t sy by arrest ofte anderssints, om daer van betaelt te worden, oft 't selve wederom te hebben. (…).'

Art. 2. 'Maer als 't selve aen eenen anderen voorts is verkocht, verhandelt oft verpandt ende gelevert oft opgedraegen, soo en heeft der eerste vercooper geen vervolgh tegens den tweeden cooper ofte crediteuren, die ter goeder trouwen, nae date van den jersten coop, den prijs betaelt ofte het geldt daer op gedaen heeft, maer blijven bij dengenen, die bij wettigen tytel daer toe is gecommen.'

46. STAwn1545

Costumen van Antwerpen 1545 ('Antiquissimae') (De Longé, Coutumes du Pays et duché de Brabant, I, 1870, 184)

Titel 4, Art. 40: 'Item als yemant syn goet vercoopt om met gereeden gelde betaelt te worden, ende tselve den coopere levert (meynende syn gelt corts daer te ontfangene), die leveringhen nyet tegenstaende blyft de vercoopere heere ende meester van dien goeden, ende moeten hem weder volghen indien hy nyet betaelt en wordt; dies moet de vercoopere (indien gevalle) syne vercochte goeden corts nae de traditie vervolghen (…).'

47. STAwn1582

Rechten ende Costumen van Antwerpen 1582 ('Impressae') (Rechten ende Costumen van Antwerpen, Plantijn 1582, 290)

Titel 58, Art. 7: 'Item degene, die syn goet vercocht ende geleverd heeft, 't sy om met gereeden gelde ofte op dach betaelt te worden, indien de cooper corts daer nae failleert, wech loopt oft hem versteect sonder betaelen, sulcs dat de rechter daer uit de quade trouwe ende bedrogh des coopers can bemercken, mach de vercooper syn goet vervolghen, arresteren, vindiceren ende syn maecken.'

48. STAwn1608

Costumen van Antwerpen 1608 ('Compilatae') (De Longé, Coutumes de la ville d'Anvers, Vol. III, 1872, 328); www.kuleuven-kulak.be/facult/rechten/Monballyu/Rechtlagelanden/Brabantsrecht/brabantsrechtindex.htm)

Art. III.3.3: '13. De gene die sijn goet vercocht ende gelevert heeft, sonder dach oft om met gereeden gelde betaelt te wordden, indijen hij daervan t'sijnder maninge oft aensoeck nijet en wort voldaen, mach t'selve goet tot sijnder versekerheijt onder den cooper altijts doen arresteren ende besetten, om sijn goet wederomme te hebben, oft van den prijs van dijen voldaen te sijn, t'sij [dat] den cooper is gebroken oft niet.

14. Ende oft den cooper t'goet aen een ander hadde vercocht, verseth oft bij anderen lastigen titel vertiert, ende dat den tweeden cooper oft vercrijger t'selve goet ter goeder trouwen hadde vercocht [gecocht] oft vercregen, totten dijen bewijsen

conste, naer date van den coop den prijs daervan betaelt, oft sijne penningen daerop geschoten, oft anderssints voldaen te hebben, soo en soude den eersten vercooper tegens den tweeden cooper geen vervolch hebben, alwaer den eersten cooper daernaer terstont gefailleert.

15. Behoudelijck dat, soo verre den vercooper op gereet gelt heeft vercocht, ende terstont selver naergaet oft ijmant seijnt om sijn gelt te ontfangen ende nijet en wordt betaelt, ende dat den cooper binnen den tijt dat den vercooper sijn goet gevoechelijck hadde mogen [doen] besetten (daertoe den vercooper wort gegunt den tijt van XXIII uren), het selve voorts vercoopt, als [den] eersten vercooper alsdan sijn goet mach vervolgen tegens eenenijgelijck, daeronder hij het vindt, tot dat hij van den prijs van dijen is betaelt.

16. Item, soo wanneer den cooper sonder dach, oft om met gereeden gelde te betaelen, heeft gecocht, ende corts daernaer, dat is binnen den tijt van veerthien daegen, compt te breken ofte sijn gelooff [crediet] te verliesen, ende dat hij ondertusschen het goet aen een ander heeft vercocht, verseth oft anderssints met lastigen titel vertiert, soo is evenwel den vercooper de naeste tot sijn goet, mits goet doende aen den vercrijger van den eersten cooper, t'gene hij daeroppe ofte voor heeft gegeven.

17. Ende oft de gene die alsulcke goet ofte coopmanschappe van den eersten cooper heeft vercregen, dat voorts hadde vercocht, ende daeraff maer [meer] gemaeckt ende vercregen dan hij daervore gegeven hadde, t'selve soude sijn tot verlichtinge van de schade van den eersten vercooper, die bij bedroge van den eersten cooper van den sijnen gebloot is.

18. Maer oft den cooper eenich goet gecocht hadde om met gereede penningen, ofte oock op dach, te betaelen, ende dat hy corts daernaer, dat is binnen vierthien daegen, alsvore, quaeme te breken [oft failleren], ende ondertusschen de selve goeden hadde gegeven in betaelinge oft versekeringe van eenige sijne voorgaende schulden aen ijmandt [eenige] van sijne crediteuren, alsdan soude den vercooper de selve goeden mogen doen arresteren, besetten ende vervolgen onder de selve crediteuren, al oft die vuijtten eersten coopers handen niet en waren gescheijden.

19. Als ijmant sijn goet heeft vercocht ende gelevert op dach, ende dat den cooper daernaer compt insolvent te wordden oft voorvluchtich, oft dat hij hem versteckt, soo mach den vercooper altijt sijn goet onder den cooper, oft in sijne macht, oft tot sijnder ordre sijnde, arresteren, besetten ende vervolgen, om daervan betaelt te sijn, oft, bij gebreke van dijen, t'selve wederomme te hebben, als voore.

20. Maer soo verre t'selve goet, op dach gecocht ende gelevert sijnde, bij den derden persoon ter goeder trouwen bij wettigen oft [ende] lastigen titel waere vercregen, alsdan en soude den eersten vercooper daerop geen vervolch hebben, maer soude sijne betaelinge, gelijck alle andere crediteuren, op sijnen cooper ende desselffs goeden moeten soecken.'

49. STDne1577

Costumen van Deurne 1577 (www.kuleuven-kulak.be/facult/rechten/Monballyu/Rechtlagelanden/Brabantsrecht/Varia/deurne.html

Art. 565: 'Item, soo wie sijn goet verkocht ende ghelevert heeft, 't zij om metghereeden gelde oft op dagh betaelt te worden, indien den cooper kortsdaernaer failgeert, wegh loopt oft hem versteeckt sonder te betalen, sulcksdat den rechter daeruijt de quade trouwe ende bedrogh des koopers kanbemercken, magh den vercooper alsdan sijn goet vervolghen, arresteren, vendiceren ende sijn maecken.'

50. STPar1580

Coutume de Paris 1580 (Feenstra 1949, 208)

Art. 176: 'Qui vend aucune chose mobiliaire sans jour et sans terme, esperant estre payé promptement, il peut la chose poursuir en quelque lieu qu'elle soit transportée, pour estre payé du pris qu'il l'a vendue.'

51. PaPa1306

Parlement de Paris 4 January 1306 (M. Beugnot (ed.), Les Olims ou Registres des arrest rendus par la cour du roi, tome III, 1, Paris 1844, 209 ff; also in Feenstra 1949, 308)

52. STMrs1253

Statuts de Marseille 1253 (Regine Pernoud, Les statuts municipaux de Marseille, Monaco 1949)

Liber III Caput VII: (...) 'de pretio... venditori non est... in solidum satisfactum' en 'si forte... emptorem... contigerit labi facultatibus suis, vel si bona eius dentur in solutum per estimatores, vel per curiam Massiliae, vel etiam si contigerit ipsum vergi ad inopiam, vel impotentiam talem quod ipse forte aut fugiat, vel latitet, vel in quaestionem vertatur, vel dubitetur an de bonis eius possit satisfieri ipsis creditoribus... veluti suam vendicare aut quasi prae omnibus aliis pro dicto pretio...'

53. STPsa1161

Constitutum usus Pisanae civitatis 1161

Titel 15: 'Cum bono debitoris, qui factus est non solvendo, creditoribus per libram conceduntur, si aliquis creditorum rem, quam ei vendidit vel alia ex causa ei dedit vel concessit, ex qua pretium vel id quod inde conventum sibi fuerat non habuerit, inter res alias debitoris invenerit, precipuam, equitatis ratione suadente, eam habet.'

54. STSna1262

Constituto del comune di Siena 1262 (Feenstra 1949, 262)
II, 77: 'Et quicumque vendiderit avere suum alcui et ei pretium non fuerit solutum, et emptor aufugerit vel suspectus vel mortuus fuisset, possit ille qui vendidit, petere et rehabere ipsum ab eo, apud quem fuerit invenctum, nisi ipse primus emptor vendidissit vel alienasset; niso hoc fecisset in fraudem.'

55. STSri1316

Statuti di Sassari 1316 (Feenstra 1949, 263)
Cap. XCI: 'Quando saet facher vendita alcuna de alcuna cosa mobile, over instabile, et issu prethu non se pachet ad presente, ma se vendet, ad termen, et cio aet apparre per iscriptura plubica de notaiu, in fina ad tantu qui assu recivitore over venditore aet esser pagatu dessa cosa vendita, non se pothat, nen deppiat molestare in cussa cosa vendita per isse per alcunu, assu quale esseret inanti su compratore de cussa cosa obligatu, ma semper se dicta cosa siat propriu pinnos de cusse qui laet vender, et quantu est in cussa siat plus forte in rathone, in fina a tantu qui aet esser ad isse integramente satisfactu dessu prethu de cussa cosa.'

56. STAbg1288

Statuti di Albenga 1288 (Gli Statuti di Albenga del 1288, Genova 1995, 276)
'et tunc presumam et habebo pecuniam et rem illam que inventa fuerit in eius bonis a tempore quo pecuniam vel rem illam acceperit ut dictum est procesisse et comperatam esse de pecunia illa vel societate vel acomodatione, nisi res illa sit illa de qua venditor nondum sit precium consecutus. In quo casu venditor habeat vendicationem rei vendite, donec sibi de precio fuerit satisfactum.'

Annex 2 List of traits*

1 Basis of recovery in: [0] ownership [1] tacit security (*pand*)/vindicatio pignoris/ *obligation spéciale* [2] fairness (*aequitas*) [3] no explicit mention [4] stoppage in transitu
2 Right can be enforced: [0] both in and outside of buyer's insolvency [1] not in case of buyer's insolvency [2] only in case of buyer's insolvency/*vlucht* [3] only in case of buyer's insolvency/*vlucht* from which the buyer's deceit can be derived [4] only in case of (commercial) buyer's insolvency and goods in transit
3 Type of goods: [0] only movables [1] movables and immovable [2] foodstuff
4 Right can be enforced: [0] not in case of credit (à contant/fidem sequi) [1] also in case of credit [2] only in case of credit
5 Time within which to claim after delivery: [0] up to 3 days (*sonder merren/binnen der voorsschen/corts*) [1] 7 or 8 days [2] 10 days [3] 14 or 15 days [4] 30 days [5] 6 weeks or 'reasonable time' [6] 6 weeks after claim is enforceable or 60 days after storage by buyer [7] 8 days, but 15 days in case of insolvent trader [8] 3 months [9] no specific statutory time limit
6 Right is also enforceable against third party possessors: [0] yes [1] not if bona fide buyer/buyer sine fraude [2] not if third party obtained from buyer against counterperformance [3] not if one year bona fide possession and sine fraude [4] only if claim is brought within 23 hours [5] no (goods must still be with buyer)
7 Sale must have been laid down in a notarial deed: [0] absent [1] present
8 Right can only be exercised if goods are in same state as when delivered: [0] absent [1] present [2] more detailed rule
9 Right can only be enforced if the goods are still in the country of delivery: [0] absent [1] present
10 In case of non-payment, a fine is to be paid by the buyer: [0] absent [1] present
11 Separate statutory regime or rule for insolvent (commercial) parties: [0] absent [1] only for goods in transit [2] only if goods are with buyer [3] yes
12 Explicit protection of buyer's creditors in good faith with a security right: [0] absent [1] present
13 The requirements for termination in case of non-performance must be met: [0] absent [1] present
14 Rights to be exercised by a written declaration: [0] absent [1] present
15 A separate right of stoppage in transit is recognised or referred to in the provision: [0] absent [1] present
16 The right cannot be enforced if the seller received satisfaction in another way than through payment of the price: [0] absent [1] present

* Traits are coded in two different ways. If traits are either present or absent (e.g. trait 7), they are coded as binary characters. Traits that can take various possible forms (e.g. trait 5: number of days within which to claim after delivery) are coded as multi-state characters. Following Tehrani 2013, in cases where a trait cannot occur because this is incompatible with the presence of other traits, the trait is coded as a gap (represented by a '-' symbol in the matrix).

Index of Names and Places

Maastricht Law Series

The Maastricht Law Series is created in 2018 by Boom juridisch and Eleven International Publishing in association with the Maastricht University Faculty of Law. The Maastricht Law Series publishes books on comparative, European and International law. The series builds upon the tradition of excellence in research at the Maastricht Faculty of Law, its research centers and the Ius Commune Research School. The Maastricht Law Series is a peer reviewed book series that allows researchers an excellent opportunity to showcase their work.

Published in this series:

Volume 1: Reinhard Zimmermann, Does the Law of Succession Reflect Cultural Differences?, ISBN 978-94-6236-856-9

Volume 2: Anna Berlee, Access to personal data in public land registers, ISBN 978-94-6236-841-5

Volume 3: Marcus Meyer, The Position of Dutch Works Councils in Multinational Corporations, ISBN 978-94-6236-848-4

Volume 4: Jaap Hage, Foundations and Building Blocks of Law, ISBN 978-94-6236-860-6

Volume 5: Bastiaan van Zelst, The End of Justice(s)?, ISBN 978-94-6236-881-1

Volume 6: Lars van Vliet & Agustin Parise (eds.), Re- De- Co-dification? New Insights on the Codification of Private Law, ISBN 978-94-6236-900-9

Volume 7: Caroline Rupp, Rafael Ibarra Garza & Bram Akkermans, Property Law Perspectives VI, ISBN 978-94-6236-904-7

Volume 8: Aalt Willem Heringa, Europees Nederlands Staatsrecht, ISBN 978-94-6290-604-4

Volume 9: Symeon C. Symeonides, The "Private" in Private International Law, ISBN 978-94-6236-949-8

Volume 10: Jaap Hage, European Integration, ISBN 978-94-6236-981-8

Volume 11: Jan M. Smits, Five Uneasy Pieces. Essays on Law and Evolution, ISBN 978-94-6236-982-5

Volume 12: Hannah Brodersen, Vincent Glerum & André Klip, The European Arrest Warrant and In Absentia Judgements, ISBN 978-94-6236-985-6

Volume 13: Bram Akkermans & Gijs van Dijck, Sustainability and Private Law, ISBN 978-94-6236-986-3
Volume 14: Antonia Waltermann, David Roef, Jaap Hage & Marko Jelicic, Law, Science, Rationality, ISBN 978-94-6236-989-4

9 789462 369825

Printed by Libri Plureos GmbH in Hamburg,
Germany